VALUES-
DRIVEN
LEADERSHIP

Books by Aubrey Malphurs

Advanced Strategic Planning
Being Leaders
Biblical Manhood and Womanhood
Building Leaders (coauthor)
Contemporary Weddings, Funerals, and Other Occasions (coauthor)
Church Next (coauthor)
Developing a Dynamic Mission for Your Ministry
Developing a Vision for Ministry in the 21st Century
Doing Church
The Dynamics of Church Leadership
Maximizing Your Effectiveness
Ministry Nuts and Bolts
Planting Growing Churches for the 21st Century
Pouring New Wine into Old Wineskins
Strategy 2000
Vision America

VALUES-DRIVEN LEADERSHIP

DISCOVERING AND DEVELOPING YOUR CORE VALUES FOR MINISTRY

SECOND EDITION

AUBREY MALPHURS

BakerBooks

a division of Baker Publishing Group
Grand Rapids, Michigan

Published by Baker Books
a division of Baker Publishing Group
P.O. Box 6287, Grand Rapids, MI 49516-6287
www.bakerbooks.com

Printed in the United States of America

Library of Congress Cataloging-in-Publication Data
Malphurs, Aubrey.
  Values-driven leadership : discovering and developing your core values for ministry / Aubrey Malphurs. —2nd ed.
      p.   cm.
  Includes bibliographical references and index.
  ISBN 10: 0-8010-6516-X (pbk.)
  ISBN 978-0-8010-6516-3 (pbk.)
  1. Church management. 2. Values. I. Title.
VB652.M3566 2004
253—dc22   2003028146

CONTENTS

INTRODUCTION

Some fifty years ago a small core of committed Christians planted Hope Community Church in Little Hope, Texas, a rural town due west of a large burgeoning city in north-central Texas. Over time the city doubled in size and intruded into what was once the quiet community of Little Hope. The growth caught the locals by surprise, as evidenced by a staccato mix of one-acre farms and older, in-need-of-repair houses located practically next door to fresh new tract homes with landscaped yards and freshly manicured Bermuda-grass lawns.

The aging local historian, a lifelong member of the church and the proprietor of a local feed store, was quick to share with anyone willing to listen how the church had seen better days. The founding pastor, Brother Fred, led the new, robust congregation, consisting mostly of farmers, ranchers, and local small-business types and their families, to a membership of 250 people. Initially some of the folks wanted to name the church after the town—Little Hope Community Church—but the wise, respected, older pastor managed to talk them out of it. Then he retired, and over the next ten to fifteen years five pastors came and went while the church membership plummeted to eighty to one hundred faithful old-timers, mixed with a slim assortment of children and grandchildren. Brother Fred cast a long shadow that none of the following pastors seemed to escape.

David Johnson, with his wife and two small children, arrived on the scene as the sixth pastor. David grew up in the Northeast, where he obtained a degree in marketing from a prestigious Ivy League school. More important, during his third year, he came to faith in Christ through an active parachurch ministry on campus. His conversion turned his life upside down. David decided to pursue ministry and met his wife,

Mary, who was also active in the campus ministry. On graduation, he enrolled at a seminary in preparation for church ministry. During the seminary years, David and Mary attended a new, contemporary, urban church that ministered to a predominantly professional and college community. The church had a national reputation for its creativity and innovation, and it attracted and reached numerous unchurched, lost people. Fresh out of seminary, David would cut his teeth on Hope Community Church. Though a bit naïve, he came with a vision—a Great Commission vision—to see lost people in the community embrace the Savior and grow to maturity in Christ.

With the intrusion of the city, new people moved to the Little Hope area and began to visit and eventually join the church. Some were Christians, but a significant number came to faith through the ministry of the church. In particular they were attracted to the unconventional ministry style of David Johnson. The membership began to swell, and soon the newcomers outnumbered the church's old-timers, which caused quite a stir. To complicate matters, new people were unknowingly occupying spaces in pews traditionally reserved for those who had contributed the funds to purchase the pews.

More important, the younger newcomers were also pressing for a more contemporary style of worship and better educational facilities for their kids. Tempers flared when a group of young mothers asked the board to renovate the nursery. As one elderly board member shared with another patriarch, "Our nursery was good enough for our kids; it should be good enough for theirs!" The old guard found little consolation from Brother David, who sided with the new people. Though he had not discussed it with the board, all this was a part of his vision for Hope Community Church.

Pastor David lasted another year before the church asked him to leave. It was not a pleasant experience. If it were not for the fact that he had such a strong vision, he would have dropped out of the ministry and pursued a career in the marketplace. The church suffered as well. Within a year most of the new people had left, and the attendance had plummeted back to eighty to one hundred people. Most of the newcomers transferred to several recently planted new paradigm churches in the area. Within another five to ten years Hope Community Church would be no more.

What went wrong? Numerous things, and we could place much blame on both sides. However, a primary missing ingredient in the candidating recipe was a discussion of core ministry values.

What David Johnson and other leaders like him must realize is that joining a ministry, any ministry, has much in common with taking a wife—it's a marriage. A wise potential husband discovers his fiancée's values before saying, "I do." He realizes that their values will shape and drive their marriage. If they begin the relationship with few common values, they are destined for much heartache and suffering and the likelihood of the painful dissolution of their relationship. Had David taken the time before the candidating process to identify and articulate his core ministry values, and had the church done the same, all would have realized during the candidating engagement that without certain major adjustments the intended marriage was going to end in a painful divorce.

Realistically, however, not many seminarians and practicing pastors have taken time to unearth and articulate their ministry values. And not many churches have busied themselves with the same. When I wrote the first edition of this book in 1996, only a few companies, which tend to be ten to twenty years ahead of the typical American church, had captured the importance of organizational core values. Tom Peters and Robert Waterman wrote, "Surprisingly . . . only a few brave business writers have taken the plunge and written about values."[1] Much has changed in the corporate context. There is much more material available on values—especially since the fall of Enron in 2000. However, little information from a Christian perspective is available for pastors or churches on this concept that is so vital to a significant ministry in the twenty-first century.[2]

At a major event in the 1990s for church leaders throughout North America, Bill Hybels, founder and senior pastor of Willow Creek Community Church, and Ken Blanchard, an author, speaker, and international business consultant, stated that twenty-first-century leaders will not lead by the authority of their position but by an ability to articulate a vision and core values of their organization or congregation. In 1992 I wrote a pioneering work, *Developing a Vision for Ministry in the 21st Century,* to provide information to help Christian leaders with the vision concept.[3] Since so little was available in the 1990s, I wrote this book to introduce and help Christian leaders with the cutting-edge concept of organizational core values. While ministry vision has been a key concern for Christian organizations in the 1990s and beyond, ministry values will be a key issue for the twenty-first century.

Organizational values exist on two levels. One is the individual level. People in general and leaders in particular have a set of core ministry values that influences much if not all that they do. The other level is the corporate or congregational level. Every ministry organization, whether church or parachurch, has a set of core values that guides what the ministry seeks to accomplish. Also other ministries that come under the umbrella of the church or parachurch have their values sets.

An understanding of an individual's or an organization's precepts is a key to an extended, successful ministry. In church planting, the point pastor's core values will become the organizational values of the future church. In church revitalization, the candidating pastor and the church need to understand not only the potential pastor's values but those of the prospective church in determining a ministry match. Some smaller churches in North America that are struggling for survival have attempted church mergers. The success of such mergers depends to a great extent on values congruence. Few if any values sets match, and few if any mergers work. The same holds true for the hiring of staff and so on.

A ministry organization's core values are at the center of its corporate culture. Every ministry, church, or parachurch has a culture, though it may not be aware of it. A church's culture consists of such things as its traditions, heroes, expectations, norms, stories, rituals, symbols, rewards, and—most important—its values. In fact these cultural ingredients revolve around the core values. A congregational culture ties its people together and gives meaning and purpose to the ministry's life. It provides a sense of identity and stability and sets boundaries. I summarize it as the way we do things around here. Increasingly, strong leaders are aware that organizations with a strong, positive, biblically based culture are consistently high-performing ministries.

A church's core values are a vital part of its character, which is also determined by its mission, vision, and strategy. Because these characteristics hold the very identity of the church, some of us refer to them as the ministry's DNA. Just as a person's DNA contains the blueprint or the building blocks of the human cell, so the church's DNA contains its blueprint. I will use the term DNA as a reference to these identity items throughout the book.

Several credos, or values statements, are provided as examples in the appendixes. Appendix A contains church credos, appendix B presents parachurch credos, and appendix C provides marketplace credos. You will be regularly pointed to all of them in general and to specific examples in particular. They will help you understand the concept of essential organizational or corporate values; aid you in discovering your own; and challenge you to develop, communicate, implement, and preserve your credo. Look over them now and periodically browse through them as you work your way through this book.

This book was written for ministry organizations in general and for churches in particular to help them realize the importance of their ministry core values, which are such a vital part of their culture. Every Christian organization, as well as its leadership, needs to bring out, dust off, discuss, refine, develop, display, and implement its predominant values if it desires to make significant spiritual impact in the twenty-first century. You will profit by reading through this book with other leaders and key decision makers in your ministry. As a team, work through the exercises at the end of each chapter.

This book consists of seven chapters arranged in a logical order. Chapter 1 answers the question, How important are core values to ministry? It presents ten reasons an organization's key values are so essential to any ministry that desires to touch lives for the Savior.

Chapter 2 answers the question, What is a core value? Exactly what are we talking about? Once a ministry understands the importance of its predominant values, it is ready for a definition. This chapter will define a core value, explain its five key ingredients, and define the various kinds of organizational values, such as personal versus organizational, actual versus aspirational, conscious versus unconscious, and so on.

Chapter 3 focuses on the discovery of core values. For most, these values already exist. The chapter will guide pastors and key church decision makers through the values-discovery process to help them surface and articulate their personal ministry values as well as those of their ministries. It includes several techniques for identifying values and audits to aid them in evaluating the values. Since the values-discovery process reveals both helpful and harmful beliefs, the chapter concludes with a section on values resolution.

Chapter 4 helps Christian organizations in the development of core values. It will assign responsibility for the development process. Then it will take leaders through a four-step process for developing a values statement, or credo, tailor-made for their ministry. The chapter provides sample value statements from church and parachurch ministries for creative insight and comparison.

A church or a parachurch organization can develop and own a perfect set of unique core values for its ministry. However, if it cannot or does not communicate them in some clear way to its constituency, it cannot expect the people to know what they are, which means the organization is not likely to survive, especially in times of turbulence. Chapter 5 discusses seventeen creative and innovative as well as traditional ways of casting core values so that people will understand and grasp them.

Chapter 6 answers the question, How does a ministry implement its aspirational values either in a new or in an established context? This chapter equips leaders to implement the new values.

Chapter 7 focuses on the protection and preservation of organizational values. As the winds of change blow hard against the ministry sail, all but its values are subject to change. This chapter teaches leaders and their organizations preventative and corrective measures that preserve key values in a time of extraordinary change.

I have included discussion questions at the end of most of the chapters in all my books. I include them as an option for those individuals who find them helpful and to facilitate discussion for those who might be reading the book as a group. I believe that if you want to get the most that this book has to offer, the discussion questions are mandatory. I have designed them to help you apply the principles to your life and ministry.

Why have I written a second edition of this book? Since writing the first edition in 1996, I have continued to learn much about values through my consulting and training ministry (The Malphurs Group) and further research. In my consulting and training ministry my learning has been primarily from a church perspective. I have also learned from discoveries made in the world of corporate research, which raises a question. Is it okay for Christians to learn from sources that may not be Christian? One source of divine revelation is what theologians call general revelation. It is God's truth found in nature, history, and other sources (Ps. 19:1–6; Acts 4:15–17; 17:22–31; Rom. 1:20–21). General revelation is based on God's common grace (Matt. 5:45), and it provides man with God's general truth, since he is the source of all truth.

Though all of the Bible is true, not all truth is found in the Bible. We may find truth in other disciplines because all truth comes ultimately from God. For example, the fields of astronomy, physics, medicine, engineering, music, and many others are based on God's general revelation. Consequently we can build buildings, find cures for diseases, send people to the moon, and do many other things based on God's truth as it operates in our universe. The specific application here is to the field of corporate leadership. And I would apply it to the research and development of leadership theories throughout history. I believe that we would be wise to study leadership research and its various theories to discern nuggets of God's truth about leadership from his general revelation. Even secular researchers can stumble on to God's general revelation, because all truth is God's truth.

1

YOU CAN'T LIVE WITHOUT THEM
THE IMPORTANCE OF CORE VALUES

Values are a vital part of any ministry's culture—the very threads that make up its organizational fabric. Lyle Schaller writes: "The most important single element of any corporate, congregational, or denominational culture, however, is the value system."[1] Had Pastor David Johnson or Hope Community Church understood this, David might not have become the pastor, and the church, though struggling, might still be in existence today. While they differed in many areas, most significantly, their views of ministry rested on different foundational beliefs. It was only a matter of time before the winds of turbulence would test and eventually collapse the organizational structure. Any church or ministry organization that overlooks the importance of core beliefs does so to its detriment. Why are values so important? They affect a ministry in numerous ways. There are ten essential reasons that core values are so important to Christian ministry:

1. Values determine ministry distinctives.
2. Values dictate personal involvement.
3. Values communicate what is important.
4. Values embrace positive change.
5. Values influence overall behavior.
6. Values inspire people to action.

7. Values enhance credible leadership.
8. Values shape ministry character.
9. Values contribute to ministry success.
10. Values affect strategic planning.

Values Determine Ministry Distinctives

God has not cut all churches or all parachurch ministries from the same bolt of cloth. Your church or ministry is different from all others. This is good because it takes all kinds of ministries to reach all kinds of people. What makes all ministries different is their organizational cultures. And as Schaller notes above, the most important ingredient in any cultural recipe is the values system.

A ministry based on clearly articulated core values drives a fixed stake in the ground that says to all, "This is what we stand for; this is what we are all about; this is who we are; this is what we can do for you." Thus values are defining. They give each organization its unique identity in the ministry world. This was true in the first century. The church at Jerusalem did not use a cookie-cutter approach when it planted numerous churches throughout Asia Minor. While these new churches all agreed on the primacy and authority of the Scriptures, they emphasized different values. The church at Corinth greatly valued the ministry of spiritual gifts. The churches in Galatia wrongly valued the observance of the Mosaic law, while the church at Ephesus valued and held to strong doctrinal teaching. What was true in the first century remains true in the twenty-first century.

All churches that exist in any community are distinctive in their ministries. Some are very traditional in their worship style, while others are more contemporary. Some focus primarily on counseling; others focus more on teaching the Bible, on evangelism, on ministry to the family, on healing, on community, on the needs of the poor, on social justice, and so on. Some belong to a particular denomination; others are non-denominational. Even those of the same denomination are distinct. The difference is their values. A careful examination of the distinctives of a ministry reveals its core values. Values are responsible for diversity; they determine ministry distinctives.

If you turn to the appendixes and read a sampling of the values statements, you will quickly catch the distinctiveness of each church before ever attending a single meeting. They tell you all about the church. For example, the values statement of Fellowship Bible Church of Dallas has seven values. The first two catch your attention and are not found in any other statements.

1. *A Philosophy of Grace*
   You cannot earn God's acceptance. He accepts you now and forever through faith in Jesus Christ. The church should not focus on guilt to motivate its members, but encourage them to live good lives from a motivation of love and thankfulness toward the Lord.
2. *A Christian Self-Image*
   You can have a positive self-image, not because of who you are in yourself, but because of what God has done for you in Jesus Christ.

The first value, a philosophy of grace, tells you that this is not a church of legalists. You will not leave the services feeling guilty over what you have or have not done the prior week. Rather, you will leave encouraged to have a good week as you serve Christ because you want to, not because you feel you have to. The motivation for service is not the dirty dozen or the nasty nine, but a love for God and thankfulness for what he has done.

The second value, a Christian self-image, surprises most readers from typical older, established churches. It communicates that this church focuses on such important issues as one's self-image. This church is here to help you learn what is right about you, not what is wrong with you; it is here to help you learn who you are in Christ.

Both values tell you that this is a special church. It is a place for the walking wounded; it is a place for those who have experienced the dark side of Christianity. And it appeals to those who do not fit or have dropped out of the more typical traditional church.

The fact that values determine ministry distinctives is of particular importance to church planting. At the end of the twentieth century, 80 to 85 percent of North American churches were either plateaued or in decline. In response, various denominations and churches caught a vision for church planting. Some decided to plant churches in areas already well populated with existing churches, such as the Bible Belt in the South. This strategy has caused some to ask, Why plant churches where so many other churches that have much in common already exist? The correct answer is that a need exists in any community for churches with different distinctives based on different primary values. The question wrongly assumes that all churches have the same values and are alike. New churches bring new values or bring fresh forms to old values, which make for broader ministry distinctives that make it possible to reach a greater number and variety of people.

Values Dictate Personal Involvement

Values help people determine their personal involvement in a particular ministry. An individual should discover if his or her core ministry values align closely with the organization's values. I call this ministry values alignment based on shared ministry values. The key question is, Do we have the same values? How close are we in what we value? Can we passionately commit to the same precepts? These questions help people find common cause that leads to ministry community.

Several ministry contexts demonstrate the importance of this concept. Far too many Christians across North America are looking for the perfect church, which, in fact, does not exist. Their search would be far more profitable, and they would experience greater satisfaction, if they looked for a church with the same or similar ministry values. People involve themselves more and last longer in a ministry if they know from the beginning that they share core values. When people walk through the church's front door clearly understanding both their own and the church's values, it promotes their assimilation, closing the church's back door.

Look again at the first two values of Fellowship Bible Church. On the one hand, the first value, a philosophy of grace, tells you that not only is this not a church of legalists, a distinctive, but it is not a church for legalists. It communicates that, if you are into legalism, this is not the church for you. On the other hand, it invites those who may have attended or ministered in abusive legalistic systems to come and experience God's forgiving, refreshing grace. The second value, a Christian self-image, woos the person with a poor self-image who may have grown up in an abusive family—Christian or otherwise—or in an abusive church. It says, Come and learn what Christ has done for you and who you really are in him.

If a pastor such as David Johnson is candidating for a particular church—in our example, Hope Community Church—both the candidate and the church would be wise to articulate and compare their primary church values as well as their ministry visions. They need to ask, Do we share the same basic core values? Is there a ministry match? Where do we agree or disagree? Do we fit together? As demonstrated in the life of Pastor David and Hope Church, this could make the difference between tragedy and triumph.

Church planters can spare themselves and their churches much grief by communicating their values to all who would become a part of the church. Communicate the primary beliefs early in the life of the new work and repeatedly throughout the life of the church. Unfortunately, new churches often attract disgruntled people with varied beliefs who come from other churches where they have caused numerous problems. The church planter must make clear to everyone the values that form the direction of the new work and encourage those with similar values to join the team, while discouraging those with different values from future involvement.

A characteristic of some North American churches from the 1980s into the twenty-first century has been the megachurch phenomenon. More large churches exist now than ever before. At the same time, smaller churches that until recently have clung so tenaciously to their existence are rapidly dying. To perpetuate their existence, some small churches are merging. The majority of the mergers, however, have proved unsuccessful. This is because they approach the merger blindly. A major reason for this failure is an unconscious disagreement over fundamental core ministry values. The key to success is the clarification, discussion, and alignment of core values. If they cannot find common cause in their primary beliefs, they must not attempt a merger.

A senior pastor should regularly discuss the church's key values with his professional and lay staff to make sure that all agree. If a staff person has any major disagreements, he or she should look for another church. When interviewing potential staff, the senior pastor must take the initiative to communicate the vision and values to determine common cause. He interviews prospective staff with an eye to how the person's values will align with those of the ministry. This action will protect both the staff and the church from the typical divisive issues that destroy so many ministries.

The common thread that runs through all these ministry contexts is the importance of shared values. A ministry's values communicate who is involved in it. A church or parachurch organization is the embodiment of the values of the men and women who give it substance. Broad diversity of precepts can fragment the organization. Therefore, successful leaders work hard at achieving consensus on basic values because shared beliefs tend to knit individual and organizational purposes together. They are an answer to Paul's prayer in Romans 15:5 for vital unity in the body of Christ. The ministry must convey its beliefs and values to those who desire to be a part of it. If the values match, most likely there will be a ministry match.

Values Communicate What Is Important

An organization's core values signal its bottom line. They dictate what it stands for, what truly matters, what is worthwhile and desirous. They determine what is inviolate for it; they define what it believes is God's heart for its ministry. While every ministry has a set of values, not all of the values are of equal importance. Some take priority over others. These high-priority values represent a watershed, or point of no return, for the ministry.

Acts 6:1–7 records a bottom-line or watershed experience in the life of a fragile early church. The twelve apostles faced a potential church split over an accusation of discrimination. The Grecian Jews complained that the Hebraic Jews were neglecting the Grecian widows in the daily distribution of food. Rather than becoming sidetracked with what for them was a low-priority value—waiting on tables—the Twelve assigned this responsibility to seven others. This allowed the Twelve to focus on the higher values of prayer and the ministry of the Word.

This truth has several practical ramifications. First, those in church or parachurch ministries often find themselves in difficult situations, and they ask themselves certain key questions: Is it time for me to leave this ministry? Is it time for me to move on to another ministry altogether? How can a leader or staff person know when it is best to stick it out or to move on? The answer is in the form of another question: Does the situation force you to compromise, deny, or abandon your fundamental ministry values? Core organizational beliefs draw the line in the sand. If your personal beliefs tempt you to step over this line, you are morally obligated to resign and look for a more compatible ministry. Core organizational beliefs are so essential to the ministry that you as a leader in that ministry should resign before violating them.

Second, every organization must have a commitment to values that matter. The organization must passionately stand for something. When this is not the case, the situation may degenerate into complaining, abuse, and ultimately ministry paralysis (as in Acts 6:1). This becomes most evident in long-term ministries that over the years have lost touch with why they are doing what they are doing. Rather than having effective ministry, they become bogged down in a quagmire of disarray, clutter, and ineffectiveness.

Third, the primary values also help everyone in the organization to know and then focus their energy on what is truly important to the ministry. High-priority values paint a target on the wall; they provide a bull's-eye for industrious people to shoot at. They tell people where to spend their time and energy most effectively, as the Twelve spent time with prayer and the ministry of the Word in Acts 6:4. Failure to communicate the organization's core values will cause people to waste their time, will create dissatisfaction, and will bring much needless frustration. This could have been the result had the Twelve decided to wait on tables in Acts 6:2. Professional and lay staff find themselves involved in ministries that they should delegate to others. Traditionally these organizations experience high personnel turnover.

Values Embrace Positive Change

More than at any other time in its history, North America is exploding with accelerating change. America and all of Western society have climbed on board the roller coaster of change only to find that they cannot climb off. And no end to the convoluted, chaotic ride is in sight.

This change is not like the transitions that we have experienced in the past. It appears to be a part of a new order breaking away from the old, an entire society moving into a new epoch. In America, the shift is from the modern to a postmodern period.[2] And the alteration is not on the surface only but goes to the core of what our very lives and organizations are all about. The early church, in Acts, faced a similar epochal transition, but the changes were not as accelerated as they are today.

The problem that all this upheaval has caused for the individual is change overload. People can handle only so much change over a short time before it leaves them feeling emotionally impotent. Rapid change can actually make people physically sick because it induces tremendous stress when it involves jobs, relatives, beliefs, and other important areas of life. Rapid change also has a deep impact on our institutions, including church and parachurch ministries, creating a sense of uncertainty of direction and a lack of clarity about the organization's future. Many churches, in particular, cannot adjust and are being quickly left behind. The problem is that when the rate of change within the church or Christian organization is slower than the change outside, the end of the organization is in sight.

The important questions for Christian ministries are, How can we know what to change in our organizations and what not to change? How can we know what is good or bad change for the organization? With the increasing speed of change, a wrong move would not only prove costly; it could prove deadly to the ministry. The only sacred cows in the ministry are its vision, its core values, and its doctrinal beliefs as based on Scripture. Its primary values provide a useful anchor in a culture that is constantly in a state of accelerating flux. The church or parachurch organization must have a set of values that provides it with a common and consistent sense of direction.

These core values serve as glue and a guiding force that hold a visionary ministry together in the midst of transition. As the culture rapidly changes around it, the organization must learn to adapt to change, but only within the context of its unchanging beliefs. How does it accomplish this? How does it choose what change to embrace and what to reject? The answer lies in the question, Does this change agree with or contradict the core values and vision of this organization?

Values Influence Overall Behavior

A ministry's key values or beliefs are the shaping force of the entire institution. They beget attitudes that specify behavior. They affect everything about the organization: the decisions made, the goals set, the priorities established, the problems solved, the conflicts resolved, and more. Someone has compared key beliefs to an ether that permeates every aspect of the institution. Schaller writes: "The values of any organization control priorities, provide the foundation for formulating goals, and set the tone and direction of the organization."[3] Values are the basis for all your behavior, the bottom line for what you will or will not do.

In the first century the Jerusalem church demonstrated on two occasions the impact that values have on behavior. The core biblical values of the Twelve in the problematic situation of Acts 6:1–7 decided a potentially explosive encounter early in the life of the young church. Later at the Jerusalem council, recorded in Acts 15, the church resolved another festering conflict. It opted for the value of grace. It decided that a Gentile does not have to become a cultural Jew to be saved. Both these monumental decisions solved major problems and resolved conflicts that set the tone and direction of the church at critical junctures in its fragile life.

Every day each one of us who serves in a Christian organization faces situations that call for significant thought, personal opinion, decision making, problem solving, and conflict resolution. Some of these situations appear routine; others are novel. Some seem relatively trivial, while others seem monumental. Regardless, an awareness of our core values helps us understand what is at the center of all this. It enables us to better understand the basis of our operations—what really makes us tick.

These beliefs are so important that they must always come before ministry policies, practices, and goals. The important lesson here is that you do not start with the latter and work back to the former; it is the other way around. Many organizations violate this principle. If you carefully examine their behavior as evidenced by their policies and practices, you will discover that they routinely violate their fundamental beliefs. For example, a church as it begins to age may genuinely desire to reach and minister to younger people such as Baby Busters and Bridgers as well as to its older members. However, it may enact a policy that limits the worship service to traditional music, whereas many Busters and Bridgers prefer a more contemporary format.

Another important issue here is understanding and predicting future behavior. Researchers in organizational behavior are concerned with understanding and predicting how people behave in organizational settings.[4] Knowing a church's core values will help you understand and, most important, predict how people—the congregation, board, and staff—will behave in a congregational setting. This has huge implications for change in a church because it gives an idea of how well a congregation will respond to intentional changes. Thus leaders will have a feel for how much change to introduce and when it is best to do so.

Values Inspire People to Action

You can tell Christians to share their faith with the lost. You can insist that they volunteer for ministry in their churches or voluntary parachurch organizations. You can offer them stipends and tease them with perks in an attempt to increase their effectiveness in what they are already doing. Yet, until they make a personal commitment to do evangelism on the local college campus or volunteer to serve in an inner-city soup kitchen, nothing much will happen. What is the missing ingredient to the recipe that stimulates and sustains this kind of transformation within a person? What moves a church member from a passive pew position to persistent participation? People need and want something they can commit to, something they feel is worthy of their best efforts. They are willing, even eager, to commit voluntarily and work for that which is truly worthwhile, that which is larger than themselves, that which creates meaning in their lives. Ministry organizations can play an enormous role in infusing their people's lives with such meaning.

The problem is that far too many ministries have missed this truth. A significant number of churches have unknowingly become killing fields of the creative spirit. To truly soar, a church must mean more than just a poorly delivered Sunday-school lecture; a reluctant guilt trip to a local retirement home; getting out the bulletin in the nick of time; scheduling an unnecessary meeting of the women's missionary society; refusing to replace a forty-year-old mimeograph; picking up trash off the lawn; updating misspelled announcements on the marquee; refinishing the varnish on worn, aging pews; refurbishing an understaffed, overpopulated nursery facility; installing a new but inferior-quality carpet in the fellowship hall; painting over some of the many water stains on the sanctuary's ceiling; or baking the most admired apple cobbler for next week's after-church potluck.

The church must somehow rise above a mediocre existence that for many has become a meaningless weekly ritual. This did not character-ize the church of the first century, and it must no longer characterize Christ's church of the twenty-first century. To truly catalyze the greatest amount of energy, to strike a resilient chord in the hearts of its people, to seize the day, a ministry must penetrate to a much deeper level. It must touch people at a level that gives their lives greater meaning and significance.

How does a ministry accomplish this? How may it play a role in infusing people's lives with meaning that, in turn, inspires them to ac-tion? The answer, as expected, has everything to do with its key beliefs or values as well as its vision. Values give servants a greater sense of meaning in their service, but not just any values and not just biblical values. The answer is shared, biblical core values. The shared beliefs of both the leaders and their followers catalyze—energize—people. They are the invisible motivators that move people's hearts toward meaningful ministry. If any Christian ministry desires to capture the great energies and gifts of its people, it must share to some degree their common core values, so that its people, in turn, find common cause with the orga-nization, which leads to authentic biblical community.

Values Enhance Credible Leadership

As the leadership goes, so goes the organization. Good leadership is essential to any successful Christian ministry. A core element in any definition of leadership is *influence;* good leaders influence people. The ability to influence followers has characterized the excellent leadership of people such as Moses, Abraham, Joshua, Deborah, Nehemiah, Es-ther, Peter, Paul, Martin Luther, John Calvin, Abraham Lincoln, Martin Luther King Jr., Elisabeth Elliot, Billy Graham, Joni Eareckson Tada, and Charles Swindoll.

In the past, bad as well as good people have influenced others. Was Adolf Hitler a leader? If the core of leadership is influence, then he was. In itself, leadership as influence is a process and is amoral. James M. Kouzes and Barry Z. Posner point out, "All processes can be used for good or evil. . . . Processes themselves are neither positive nor negative. People give processes their charge."[5] Though leadership is an amoral process, it is the leader who is decidedly moral or immoral. As leaders, Hitler was immoral; Abraham Lincoln was moral. What does this tell us? The difference between the two was their values. Thus leaders' values make all the difference in the kind of influence they exert.

All leaders are values driven, and the ministries they build are expressions of their values. Because they identify closely with their organizations and because they have committed so much of themselves to those ministries, the latter reflect their key, vital beliefs or values. Therefore, leaders must decide what they stand for. They must determine their bottom line. Not just any bottom line will do. It is imperative that Christian leaders opt for a strong Bible-based values system. This is because strong beliefs make for strong leaders, and strong leaders make for strong ministry organizations.

When leaders have chosen a core set of values for their organizations as well as for themselves, it is equally important that they model a lifestyle consistent with these values. This is key to leadership credibility. Leaders shape people's values, and they instill these values more through what they do than through what they say. If their behavior is consistent with their values, they infuse their leadership with large doses of credibility. If, however, their walk does not match their talk, if they articulate one set of values for the organization but operate with a different set, followers will view them as hypocrites, and they will lose all credibility. Regarding the business world, Amy Edmondson writes, "When employees sense that a leader's decisions are at odds with company values—even when they're not—they are quick to conclude that the leader lacks personal commitment to the values. He's seen as a hypocrite."[6] In 1 Timothy 4:12 this is made very clear to Timothy, a young leader and mentor of leaders, when Paul writes to him: "Don't let anyone look down on you because you are young, but set an example for the believers in speech, in life, in love, in faith and in purity." In 1 Corinthians 11:1 he writes to the Corinthian church: "Follow my example, as I follow the example of Christ."

Values Shape Ministry Character

A person's character, whether good or bad, directly affects how he or she conducts life. People of poor character tend to live life poorly in that they may fudge on the truth or cut corners to accomplish their goals. People of good character live life well in that they are honest, moral, and upright. In either case it is their values that directly affect their characters. A person's character is the direct descendent of his or her values; personal character rests on the foundation of personal values.

The same is true for any ministry organization. Its values are character defining. Core values are the qualities that make up and establish an organization's character, and that character determines how the organization conducts its ministry or business. It is essential that the captain of a jumbo jet have a vision of where the plane is going and a strategy for how it will get there. However, he and the rest of the crew must understand that the passengers and the general public will use certain standards to judge their performance before, during, and even after the trip. It is actually the character of both the entire crew and the airline that is being judged, and key to their character are their core precepts.

One of the most powerful ways that values affect the character of an organization is in its ethics. The Johnson and Johnson Company, the maker of Tylenol products, serves as an excellent example from the marketplace. It responded to an episode of product tampering by voluntarily taking all of its Tylenol capsules off the shelf—at a cost exceeding a hundred million dollars. The reason the company acted so quickly and ethically is because of its deep commitment to its credo (values set), in particular the first statement, which says, "We believe that our first responsibility is to our customers."[7]

Christian organizations may consist of people who minister ethically or unethically. Unfortunately, one of the reasons so many unbelievers and unchurched people are so cynical toward Christianity and skeptical of the church is because of questionable or bad ethics on the part of certain organizations that claim to be Christian.

In the late 1980s the media announced numerous accounts of television evangelists and church pastors who entangled themselves in illicit sexual affairs and in extortion. The names and pictures of unethical exploits by preachers such as Jim Bakker and Jimmy Swaggart regularly greeted readers as they opened their morning papers or viewers as they watched the evening news. If these things were true of some of televangelism's superstars, people wondered if it were true of others in Christian service as well. Unfortunately this proved to be accurate. The breakdown in values stained not only the personal character of Christian workers, but the character of their ministries in particular, as well as Christianity in general. This is most unfortunate because it casts a dark shadow over the majority of Christian institutions that base their ministries on strong biblical values, operate on high ethical standards, and have leaders who are men and women of excellent character.

Another way that core values affect the character of an institution is in its commitment to excellence. Scripture teaches a theology of excellence, as found in Old Testament worship. God instructed the people of Israel to sacrifice their best animals (Lev. 22:20–22; Num. 18:29–30). The New Testament teaches that Christians should do their work with sustained excellence as if they were working for the Lord (Eph. 6:5–8; Col. 3:23–24). However, an organization may conduct its ministry with sustained excellence or with mediocrity—it has a choice. A church may choose to use its best musicians and vocalists to minister during its worship services, or it may choose to use anyone who claims to play an instrument or professes to carry a tune—such as Aunt Harriet's eight-year-old nephew, Fred, who has never sung on key in his brief life. Some churches' lawns are well manicured, and their facilities are very attractive and well kept. Others ignore overgrown, weed-infested yards, while their facilities are run-down and in desperate need of a fresh coat of paint. Both examples comment on the character of the church positively or negatively.

Values Contribute to Ministry Success

Any organization, Christian or non-Christian, must have and adhere to a sound set of fundamental beliefs if it is to achieve success. It is the organization's ingrained understanding of its core values more than its technical skills that makes it possible for its people to have a successful ministry.

But what is success? What makes a ministry organization successful? Success is the accomplishment of the ministry's mission and vision (Matt. 28:19–20) without compromising its vital, bottom-line values. A church that is winning lost people in its ministry community and is moving its new converts and older converts toward maturity—Christlikeness—while maintaining its distinctive, primary biblical values is successful because it is accomplishing its vision without sacrificing its core values.

Why do primary values have such a powerful effect on ministry performance? The answer lies in several factors. First, when people flesh out their beliefs in service, they will impact the commitment, enthusiasm, and drive of others in the organization, making it a powerful force in its community. For example, Christians who regularly evangelize lost people inspire others to model their behavior.

Second, shared values create within people the incentive to serve for longer hours and accomplish harder, more careful ministry. A community of believers, united by a common cause, is enthusiastic and committed and exerts a strong influence on its ministry constituents. This was the key to the effectiveness of the early church (see Acts 2:42–47; 4:32–37).

Third, congruent values can also lower ministry costs. In the church they bring to the ministry a sense of meaning that attracts skilled, competent laypeople and relieves the need to employ large numbers of professional staff. The staff responsible for worship at Willow Creek Community Church in South Barrington, Illinois, discovered early in their ministry that by valuing excellence in worship, they attracted laypeople who were highly skilled musicians and vocalists. The values themselves are also a form of compensation that attracts more highly skilled and experienced people to serve as leaders, teachers, vocalists, and so on. For example, the miracle of a new spiritual birth—the conversion experience—which is a value in itself, is the highest form of compensation for individuals who share their faith.

Fourth, when serving a worthwhile, meaningful purpose, people become intensely committed to ministering to other people's legitimate physical and spiritual needs, as in Acts 2:44–45; 4:32–36; 6:1–4. This is the bedrock of lay mobilization in the church or parachurch organization. This is critical because in North America approximately 10 to 20 percent of the people are doing 80 to 90 percent of the ministry.

Fifth, by generating deeper personal commitment and mobilizing more people for the ministry, shared beliefs lead to much greater creativity and innovation. This, in turn, discourages the maintenance mentality that has plagued so many ministry organizations in the last two decades. People who achieve major ministry breakthroughs, such as leading a lost friend to Christ or seeing a couple's marriage healed, become totally immersed in what they are doing. And this commitment carries them through the ministry downturns, when they experience opposition and failure.

Sixth, when those who make up a ministry community own a set of key values, such as trust, fairness, integrity, and the dignity and value of people, they, in turn, greatly facilitate the accuracy and quality of communication (see Acts 5:1–11; 6:7; 15:27), the integrity of the decision-making process (see 6:2–7; 15:1–29), and the professional leader's ability to evaluate the staff and their individual ministries. People are willing to take more risks when they believe that leaders will treat them with dignity and fairness (see 15:25–26).

Values Affect Strategic Planning

Strategic planning enables the church to think and act purposefully, and this will be key to its survival in the fast-paced, change-overwhelmed twenty-first century. Strategic thinking and acting involve such activities as discovering the church's core values, developing a mission and vision, designing a strategy, and implementing that strategy. If you desire to know more about strategic planning, see my book *Advanced Strategic Planning: A New Model for Church and Ministry Leaders.*[8] While consulting and training with various churches, I have discovered that core values affect the entire strategic-planning process. Rather than attempt to show how they affect each concept of strategic thinking and acting, I will focus on one concept—vision.

A church's primary beliefs play a major part in determining its ministry vision. They guide the selection of the vision in a variety of ways. First, the key values influence the answers leaders give to the vision question. A vision has everything to do with the organization's direction. It determines where the ministry is headed. Many churches have no answer for the vision question. They have no idea where they are going; they are not aware that they even need a vision or a particular direction. While they have core values, the values are somewhat vague, diverse, and have never been clearly articulated. Hence, these churches have no focus. Other churches have multiple visions—they are attempting to move in several directions at the same time. This is a problem of competing core values. One board member prioritizes evangelism, another Bible teaching. Finally, some churches have a single, clear vision—only it is the wrong vision. They may value only the children's ministry, a counseling ministry, or the feeding of the poor, and one of those values, rather than the Great Commission, becomes the sole vision.

The Scriptures tell us what our vision should be. It is the Great Commission as recorded in Matthew 28:19–20; Mark 16:15; and Acts 1:8. The answer for a parachurch ministry lies somewhere within the Great Commission, as these organizations tend to specialize in some ministry niche that fits under the umbrella of the commission. They specialize in such areas as discipleship, evangelism, counseling, Christian education, publishing Christian material, ministering to the inner city, and so on.

Second, primary beliefs or values guide how leaders evaluate and use information that affects vision selection. This information includes a variety of things. The ministry will target people. But what kind of people? Will they be lost or saved, Baby Boomers, Busters, or Bridgers, churched or unchurched, white or Hispanic, affluent or poor? What kind of methods will the ministry employ to reach these people? Will we go door-to-door? Is marketing a legitimate method for a Christian organization? Will we advertise in the newspaper? The answers to all these questions and more will provide information that directly affects the vision. Ministries that emphasize and value the Scriptures attempt to use them as an authoritative grid through which they filter all information that will ultimately affect the choice of the vision.

Third, the primary values determine which potential visions will be considered. A Christian counseling ministry strongly values people. It believes that people matter to God. Its vision focuses on their spiritual-emotional healing. A church's vision would include this value, but it would be much broader. The values that the counseling ministry of the church hold make up the primary criteria for their limiting and selecting one vision from among several potential visions.

Finally, values determine whether the organization's constituency will accept a particular vision. The crucial factor here is shared values. It is possible for the leaders of a ministry to select and develop a vision, based on a set of values that their constituency does not share. Consequently, the leadership will be moving in one direction while the followers are moving in a different direction or are not moving at all. Should they attempt to follow the leader's vision, without sharing the vision, the results will be insipid at best.

Questions for Reflection and Discussion

1. Can you think of some additional reasons a ministry's core values are important? What are they?
2. What is distinctive about your ministry or church? What are the values that determine these distinctives?
3. Why did you choose your ministry or church over others? Are you personally involved in some ministry of your church? Why? If you are involved, what role did your core values play in that involvement?
4. Most ministries stand for something. What does yours stand for? Can you articulate the values that undergird your ministry? What are they?
5. Evaluate how your church or your parachurch ministry is handling change. What is changing? What is not changing? Are the vision and the primary values changing?
6. How do your organization's values affect its ministry? Do the problems solved, the conflicts resolved, the decisions made, and the goals set reflect the organizational values?
7. Is your ministry organization growing, plateaued, or in decline? How do its values affect this situation?
8. As a leader, can you articulate your core ministry values? If yes, what are they? Do you and your ministry team share the same values? Is your performance consistent with the values you profess (do you "walk your talk")?

2

WHAT ARE WE TALKING ABOUT?
THE DEFINITION OF CORE VALUES

Because an organization's ministry values are extremely important, we must stop and ask some key questions: What are values in general, and what are core values in particular? What exactly are we talking about? The topic is new to most ministries. If Pastor David Johnson had asked the board of Hope Community Church for a statement of their primary organizational values, he would have needed to define the term. If the board had brought in a church consultant to help them discover and articulate their core values, he or she would have been wise to begin with a definition of the term. Often in defining a new concept, it helps to clarify what it is not as well as what it is.

What Core Values Are Not

People have confused several concepts with core values or have even used the terms synonymously.

Values Are Not Vision

Vision is one concept that gets confused with core values. For example, a reporter in an article in the *Washington Post* confused Johnson and

Johnson's values statement (credo) with their mission (vision) statement.[1] While the two terms are often used in the same breath, they are different in at least four ways.

First, a vision answers the question, *What* are we going to do? It gives the ministry its direction; it announces to all where it is going. Christ has already given a vision to the church; it is the Great Commission.

Core values answer the question, *Why* do we do what we do? They supply the reasons behind our vision, or what we do. While evangelism may be the vision of a parachurch ministry, it could be one of a church's core values under the umbrella of the Great Commission vision.

Second, an organization is vision focused and values driven. Because a vision is directional, it serves to focus an organization's direction. When a ministry knows its direction, it is able to focus its attention and the energies and efforts of its people. A vision functions much like a telescope. It brings the distant horizon—the destination—into clear view. Values drive the ministry. They are the reason behind each decision made, each problem solved, and each goal set. The vision clarifies the destination; the values propel the ministry toward that destination.

Third, a ministry will have values, but it may not have a vision. Far too many ministries are not aware of the importance of articulating a clear vision that provides a focused direction. Thus a large number are plateaued or in decline and find themselves locked into a maintenance mode with a museum mentality. Whether a ministry has a vision or not, it will have primary values, both good and bad. Values precede and determine actions. To understand a ministry's actions, uncover its beliefs.

Finally, a vision focuses on the future; values look to the present or the past. A ministry develops and casts—communicates—its vision for the future. It is a mental picture of what tomorrow will look like. It is a focused view of the ministry's preferred future. In an important way, visionary leaders play a primary part in determining their future and that of their ministry organizations. When they know precisely where they are going, the chances are good that they will get there.

Values deal primarily with the past and the present. Every ministry has a current set of values that are its actual precepts. They have also had values in the past that may be the same or different from their present values. Most church plants start with an outward focus because evangelism is a core value. Over time, however, they tend to turn inward and either lose that value or replace it with another. You must build an organization on the values that the people already embrace, not on what you hope they will embrace in the future.

Values Are Not Strategies

A second concept that some confuse with a value is a strategy. The vision question asks, *What* are we doing? The answer for the church is the Great Commission. A strategy answers the question, *How* are we going to do it? One answer in the early church was Paul's three missionary journeys (see Acts 13–14; 15:36–18:22; 18:23–21:16). A strategy articulates a plan for accomplishing the vision. Again, a value answers the question, *Why* are we doing what we are doing? While this concerns the vision, we may ask the same question of the strategy, Why did we choose to do it this way? Values affect which strategy a ministry uses to implement its vision.

Values Are Not Doctrinal Statements

A doctrinal statement can also be confused with a values statement. A doctrinal statement consists of a ministry's theological or doctrinal beliefs based on the Bible. If you want to know what the ministry believes about God, the Bible, Christ, the Holy Spirit, angels, man, salvation, or the future, read its doctrinal statement.[2] If you want to know what key precepts drive the ministry, read its values statement or credo. A few items may appear in both. Some credos, for example, state that the ministry is committed to the Scriptures or to relevant Bible exposition. They go on to explain that the Bible is God's inspired Word and so on. A similar declaration may be found in its doctrinal statement.

What Are Core Values?

The standard definition for a value that is commonly referenced by researchers is that of Milton Rokeach. He proposes that a value is an enduring belief that a specific mode of conduct (way of behaving) or end state of existence (such as peace or prosperity) is personally or socially preferable to an opposite or converse code of conduct or end state of existence.[3] This definition is too cerebral to be a working definition for many leaders. Consequently, I define a church's core values as its constant, passionate, sacred core beliefs that drive its ministry.[4] This definition has five important elements.

Values Are Constant

The United States is exploding with accelerating change that is without precedent in its history. Unlike other transitions in the past, a new order is breaking in on the old as we move from the modern into the postmodern era. The result is turbulent times that affect the social, economic, political, and technological arenas of the country.

In an article written in 1993, Frank Withrow indicated that knowledge doubles every two years.[5] The World Futures Society's 1994 annual conference stated that human knowledge would double every seventy-three days by the year 2020.[6] Half of what you learn today will either change or no longer be relevant in five to seven years. For example, the development of the computer, much like the printing press, has revolutionized the world. Much of this is due to the invention and unprecedented advancement of the thumbnail-sized silicon chip. In 1958 a manufacturer could place ten electronic components on one chip. By 1970 he could fit one hundred components on the same chip. Then in 1972 this number grew to one thousand, and by 1974 it was ten thousand. Today a modern computer performs millions of calculations in the time it takes a person to blink.

Most theories have assumed an exact and ordered approach to reality and commonly view all this change as an aberration. Chaos theory, however, looks at this change and the ensuing chaos as a given. It assumes that from now on, a constant state of change will characterize all complex systems. It argues that leaders must accept unpredictability and chaotic change as the new reality and plan accordingly.

The important question then is, How should Christian organizations respond to cataclysmic change? Typically, churches have assumed the position of the ostrich and, with heads buried in the sand, have ignored change as long as possible. The problem for them, as well as for the ostrich, is that they are most vulnerable. Far too many evangelical churches have assumed that any change is bad and leads to theological liberalism. They are out of touch with contemporary society by as much as ten to thirty years. Indeed, some have only just recently discovered the computer.

Accelerating change will bury institutions that ignore it. A church does not have to worry about accommodating theological liberalism if it is well into the late stages of organizational rigor mortis. Instead, it must view change from a different perspective. While some change is bad for the institution, some can be good. Most organizations that use a computer view it as essential for word processing and other critical functions such as lay mobilization. Many puzzle over how they survived so long without one.

The problem is knowing how to discern good change from bad, knowing what change will help the ministry and what will hurt it. The question is, What should and should not change around here? Also, the Christian leader is both the target of change and the ministry's agent of change, an extremely difficult role under any circumstances. The church of the first century and its leaders, as it moved from law to grace, had to face change much as the church of the twenty-first century does. The puzzle of change is not unfamiliar to Christ's church.

The answer to what should and should not change lies in an organization's core ministry values. The Jerusalem church owned and modeled a clear set of core values (Acts 2:42–47), and these values provided for them a constant in an environment constantly in flux (see appendix A). What proved true for the first-century church proves true for the twenty-first-century church. The church's vision, vital values, and basic doctrines must remain constant. They should never change. However, the forms that these constants take (small groups, crusade evangelism, and so on) are always up for change and often do change so that the organization can minister relevantly to its culture.

All of this assumes that the organization's leaders have a constant set of core ministry values, biblical or otherwise. Most do, whether or not they can articulate them. However, all leaders go through a process of values formation when these beliefs may be in a state of flux. This is true when future leaders attend a Bible college or theological seminary. A good theological program helps its students discover and develop their core values. It forces them to confront issues and exposes them to other ministry paradigms of which they may be unaware. They question old values as they examine new values. Some values remain the same; others die a silent death and are replaced. The student should graduate from Bible college or seminary having discovered his or her primary values and knowing how to discover the values of a prospective ministry organization.

Eventually, however, the leader's and the organization's central beliefs become relatively fixed. I use the term *relatively* because some slight change may take place over time. Good leaders are learners, and they will constantly evaluate new ideas and new ministry paradigms that lead to some change even in values. But when they have completed theological preparation and have had some exposure to and good involvement in an excellent ministry paradigm, their core values will be pretty well set. They do not drift with the latest trends and fashions of the day.

Values Are Passionate

Passion is a feeling word. It is felt when you care deeply and feel strongly about something. A good core value touches the heart and elicits strong emotions. It moves you all the way down to the tips of your toes. It stirs feelings that excite you and motivate you to action.

Any value can be intellectual. It can appeal and make sense to the mind. However, a core value has an additional component—it is passionate; it affects what you feel as much as what you think. It involves not only what you believe but how deeply you believe it. When leaders look over a list of beliefs, such as those found in the appendixes, they may be able to agree to some extent with most if not all of them. A person's core beliefs, however, are the ones that grab hold of the heart as well as the head. They are the ones that stand out and demand a second look. They seem to jump off the page. They have a way of touching something deep inside that the others do not.

People who share your values feel the same way about them as you do. If they hear you articulate them in a meeting, they connect with you on a gut level. They quickly sense a kindred spirit; your ministry attracts them. Those values penetrate to the bone and override any differences of opinion these people may have with you.

To fulfill a passion is to act on deeply held feelings. A core value does more than stir your emotions—it arouses you to action. It is inspirational. There is a sense that you must do something. If I feel strongly that people really matter to God, then I must share Christ with my neighbor this week. If the truth that unborn babies are human and created in the image of God touches me deeply, then I will do everything within my power to encourage their delivery into this world, including the provision of a place where an unwed mother can live until she has her child. The Jerusalem church valued fellow believers over material possessions; consequently, "they shared everything they had" (Acts 4:32).

A good leader's values move him or her to action. He or she cannot shelve a good set of values or stuff them into some church filing cabinet labeled *V.* Peter's passion for evangelism moved him to share his faith both publicly (Acts 2:14–40; 3:12–26) and privately (see Acts 10). In addition, leaders must realize that if their values do not challenge them, it is not likely that they will challenge their people either. They really do not have a set of core values because, according to our definition, people are passionate about their core values. Leaders, then, must search for and discover what really matters to them and motivates them to make a difference.

Values Are Sacred

All values are either sacred or secular. The difference is their source. Sacred values are sourced in God and may also be found in his Word. While the Bible contains sacred values, not all sacred values are found in the Bible. That is why I use the term *sacred* instead of *biblical*. Secular values are sourced neither in God nor in his Word and are not, therefore, true.

From the Middle Ages to the present, the church and the community of faith have misunderstood and misused the term *secular*. They have created a false dichotomy based on the biblical distinction between the church and the world (human society as organized against God; Latin, *saeculum*). During the Middle Ages, society associated the religious life with the ministry or the monastic life. What the monastic orders governed and owned, such as property, was sacred; what they did not control was secular. They called the priests who worked outside the church—the parish priests—"secular priests." They considered the godly life of earning a living and caring for a family in worship and service to God as "in the world" or secular.

Today many believe that whatever takes place within the church is good and sacred, but that which takes place outside the church is bad and secular. Thus the business world and the world of science are highly suspect. Many consider the idea that the marketplace could offer something to the church as sacrilege. If they were consistent, they would not use architects, engineers, or carpenters to design and build their church facilities. Neither would they use methods learned in the business world for keeping their books, training leaders, developing teams, solving problems, and so on. And they would not frequent the offices of medical doctors or dentists.

When God created the world, no sacred/secular dichotomy existed—all of God's creation was sacred (Gen. 1:31). For humankind the secular realm came into existence in Genesis 3:4, when Satan spoke the lie: "You will not surely die." Eve believed him rather than God, and the rest is ugly history. Therefore, I define the secular as that which is not under the lordship of Christ. The secular realm refers to those areas of thought and life that are not under the control and influence of authentic, biblical Christianity (1 John 2:15–17).

What takes place in the church is not automatically sacred. It may be sacred or secular, depending on motive and controlling influence. Some well-meaning Christians have assumed that everything the church has done over the ages, its traditions and practices, is right. However, the descriptions of the churches of Sardis and Laodicea, in Revelation 3, loudly protest this. Also, the church-sponsored Crusades and Inquisition provide a painful, historical contradiction; they proved to be secular.

Satan is responsible for true secularism. He controls the secular world and much of what takes place in it (Eph. 2:1–3). He is the father of lies (John 8:44), and what takes place in the secular realm is based on a lie. Thus secular values, no matter how subtle, insignificant, or innocent, are false values and harmful to any organization, Christian or not. A church may value keeping its control in the hands of a few trusted old-timers. If the motive is to prevent a younger generation of Christians from changing things—to maintain the status quo—then it may be secular and wrong. Indeed, whatever the church does, if it is not done in faith as to the Lord, it is sin (Romans 14).

Sacred values are different. They are sourced in God. God is true (Rom. 3:4) and Jesus Christ is the truth (John 14:6). Furthermore, God is immutable (Mal. 3:6; James 1:17). Therefore, he will always remain true. Whatever is sourced in God and Christ is immutable truth. The Scriptures are sourced in God and are, therefore, true (John 17:17). Any organization that names the name of Christ—that professes to be Christian—must base what it does on divine truth.

The core values contained in a Christian organization's credo should be sacred, and the true test of a values statement is, Is it sacred? That does not mean that it has to be found in the Bible. It does mean, however, that it should not contradict the Scriptures. We must ask each other, Does it agree with the Bible? While all the content of the Bible is true, not all truth is found in the Bible. For example, scientists have discovered the truth that if people brush and floss their teeth on a regular basis, they will have fewer cavities. They have also found that cigarette smoking is harmful to your health. Neither truth is found in the Bible, yet few would challenge their validity. The point is that all truth is ultimately God's truth. The problem lies in discerning truth from error in the domain of general revelation (God's knowledge as found not in the Bible but in his creation: nature, science, and history). When Scripture addresses a topic, we have God's truth on the matter. But how do we know God's truth in matters that Scripture does not address, such as the brushing of one's teeth and cigarette smoking? When dealing with knowledge based on general revelation, Christian leaders and their organizations must proceed with caution.

Therefore, a values statement could contain true values that are not in the Bible. This would probably be the values statement of an organization in the marketplace, such as a hardware store, an electronics

ment is not found in the Bible, but the underlying principle of fulfilling
responsibility is part of God's truth.

Values Are Core Beliefs

People use various synonyms for values: *precepts, choices, ideals,
assumptions, principles,* or *standards.* A study of values concerns your
beliefs, but not just any beliefs. Values are rooted in your core or central
beliefs.

A concept that all good definitions of leadership have in common
is influence. Influence assumes followers. It is said that you can call
yourself a leader. However, if you look behind you and discover that
no one is following, you are not a leader. Whether for good or for bad,
leaders influence followers.

One important way to attract and influence followers is to communicate your constant, passionate beliefs. God makes people in such a
way that they want to believe in something worthwhile, something significant. Everyone has some kind of belief system, good or bad, rational
or irrational. People will follow your leadership if you communicate to
them something in which to believe. This should not pose a problem
for the Christian leader.

But what is a belief? What is involved in a belief that is synonymous
with a value? A *belief* is a conviction or opinion that you hold to be true
as based on limited evidence or proof. It is something that you trust, or
have faith in (see Heb. 11:1). A belief is not a fact, by definition. A fact is
a conviction that a significant number of people hold to be true, based
on fairly extensive evidence. The difference is in the number of people
who hold a conviction and the amount of evidence that authenticates
the conviction.

The beliefs that make up a Christian organization's values statement
are those that affect how the ministry functions. They are not necessarily the ministry's moral values, although they should be moral. Neither

should we equate them with a ministry's doctrinal statement, though some of the contents may be similar.

Leaders of organizations hold numerous beliefs. You can get some idea of the number by looking at those provided in the organizational value statements in the appendixes. It is possible that one leader could hold to all the beliefs listed in those value statements; however, not all would be his or her core beliefs. The core beliefs are those that are essential to his or her philosophy of ministry. They are what the leader believes is God's heart for his or her ministry; they are innermost or central to the organization. While leaders carry a number of different values as part of their leadership repertoire, not all of them are high priority. The primary, essential core values are the ones at the top of the leader's priority list.

Values-Defining Elements

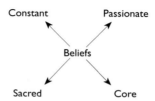

Sometimes churches find it most difficult to determine a core set of values. This is not good. According to research it is a sign of a weak culture. Charles O'Reilly states, "If there is not substantial agreement that a limited set of values is important in a social unit, a strong culture cannot be said to exist."[7] He would define a strong culture as one that holds intensely and broadly to a limited set of values.[8]

Values Drive the Ministry

The organization's central beliefs are the driver sitting behind the wheel of the ministry car. While a ministry is vision focused, it is values driven. The primary beliefs are the ministry's shaping force; they influence much if not all that it does as well as how it does it. They guide all that the ministry seeks to accomplish and define how everyone accomplishes it. They comprise the bottom line for what the institution will and will not do; they are the deeply ingrained drivers behind all of its behavior. This includes such vital areas as decision making, direction and goal setting, conflict resolution, ministry satisfaction, ministry commitment, problem solving, priorities determination, and risk taking.

DECISION MAKING

Ministries make hundreds of decisions at various levels of the organization every day. They have to say yes to some and no to others. In a time of accelerating transition, it is difficult to say wait. To put off a decision only adds to change chaos and could mean ministry disaster.

How can the ministry know what is the correct or incorrect decision? While some decisions are clear, the majority are not, which makes it very difficult for the leaders who have to make them. Leaders will find the answer to this dilemma in their core values. Virtually all decisions are rooted in them. When it is time to make a decision, the leadership responsible for the decision will make it based on the ministry's articulated core values. Research on values congruence affirms that values occupy a significant role in individual and organizational decision making.[9] The leadership will regularly ask, How do our stated values, either for the ministry as a whole or for a particular area within the ministry, affect our decision? The ministry that develops a clear set of values, shared by the ministry team, will make better decisions than the ones that have not developed their values set. With a clear set of values, the ministry team will clearly understand and share why they have done what they have done. The twelve apostles based the decision in Acts 6:1–4 on their shared values. Prayer and the ministry of the Word were high-priority precepts. Thus they decided not to spend their time waiting on tables.

This is not to say that those who have not articulated their central beliefs will not make decisions based on them—they will. However, they may not be consciously aware of what they are doing, and they may not be aware that while some of their values are helpful, others are extremely harmful to the ministry. In addition, they may be unconsciously making decisions with which the rest of the team does not agree. Decisions based on unshared values may be good decisions, but those responsible for carrying out the decisions may respond with bad attitudes and poor execution.

DIRECTION AND GOAL SETTING

As I have said, every Christian ministry should have a single, clear vision statement that focuses its direction. The vision statement creates a picture in the minds of the participants of what the ministry will look like as it accomplishes its vision. The ministry should also have a mission statement. It is essentially the same as the vision statement, but it is a planning tool, not a seeing tool. It is key not to the casting of the vision but to the planning that must take place if the organization is to accomplish its vision. Vision and mission comprise the church's direction. They dictate where the church is going. Schaller affirms that it is the values that set the tone and direction of the organization.[10]

A vital part of every planning document is a set of organizational goals. The document begins with the mission statement, followed by a set of goals and the objectives that will accomplish those goals. The key element in determining the goals is allowing the core values to dictate what is important and unimportant to the plan. The core values function as signposts to guide the organization to the realization of its goals. Indeed, Schaller notes that the church's values provide the very foundation for formulating goals.[11]

CONFLICT RESOLUTION

Every day of its life, an organization experiences conflicts of one sort or another. Conflict thrives where there is misunderstanding, anger, criticism, pride, disagreement, stubbornness, personal attacks, or intimidation. Unfortunately, this can be true of Christian organizations as well as those that are non-Christian. It characterized the churches at Corinth (1 Cor. 1:10–17) and Philippi (Phil. 4:2) in the first century, along with others. James had to address this problem with the twelve tribes scattered among the nations. He writes: "What causes fights and quarrels among you?" (James 4:1). Therefore, it should not shock us that conflict characterizes the churches of the twenty-first-century world.

What are the causes for this conflict? James identifies some of the causes in James 4:1–3. While several sources exist, the underlying source of conflict is values. James's audience valued fighting and quarreling more than turning to God and asking for what they wanted in life. Many interpersonal conflicts are the result of a conflict in values, and they are some of the most difficult to manage. An organization's values drive what it does or does not do. They determine what motivates its people and all who are in the ministry constituency. One group in the church may value evangelism over everything else; another may give the children's programs preeminence.

To resolve conflicts, the ministry needs to view behavior as the result of a set of essential driving values. If you are able to bring to the surface and clarify the values fueling the conflict, you are well on your way to resolving the conflict or to determining if a resolution is even possible. In most cases, the people in the organization do not share congruent values. The ministry has not articulated and gained allegiance to its core values. Consequently, its people either disagree directly with its values or disagree among themselves over their private values. Understanding how the beliefs of different groups empower conflict will help you to better manage conflict as it occurs.

Research clearly reveals that congruent values are the solution to conflict.[12] When people in a ministry agree and share the same values, conflict is significantly reduced.

Ministry Satisfaction

As I travel and work with congregations and their leaders, I find that not many are satisfied with their ministry in the church. There are several reasons. One is that many leaders are ministering in areas that do not use their gifts and abilities. Another is that about 20 percent of the people in the church are doing 80 percent of the ministry. However, when people are ministering in churches that don't share their values, they feel that they're not accomplishing what they could. There is a sense that they are working at cross-purposes.

Research done by Bruce Megliano and others reveals that when workers' values agree with those of their supervisors, the result is higher levels of job satisfaction.[13] Randy Boxx and others agree, finding that values congruence results in greater job satisfaction and cohesion.[14] What this means is that people in the church (congregants, boards, and staff in particular) will be more satisfied and fulfilled in their various ministries when their values are in significant alignment with the church.

Ministry Commitment

A common characteristic of church attendees in the twenty-first century is a lack of commitment to the church and its ministry. The result is that people come and they go. If this is not bad enough, the same can be said of pastors—they come and they go too. One writer observes that a major problem facing contemporary Christianity is pastoral turnover.[15] George Barna has found that the term of the average pastorate in America is only four years.[16] When a pastor lasts for an average of only four years, very little ministry of significance can take place. Congregants tend not to trust and follow the pastor, because they anticipate that he will soon move on.

Research reveals that people who share core values with a ministry are more willing to make personal sacrifices, they perform above normal expectations, and they will not leave the organization for their own self-interests.[17] I strongly advise those who take my pastoral leadership classes at Dallas Seminary and pursue pastoral ministry to check the alignment of their values with those of any potential church ministry positions, because I have observed that those who commit to a church and stay the longest are those whose values align with the values of their congregation.

PROBLEM SOLVING

It is said that you can be sure of two things in this life: death and taxes. Christian as well as non-Christian organizations would add problems to that list. If every ministry faces some conflict every day of its life, then it faces numerous problems as well. It confronts such problems as interpersonal conflict, cash flow, decline, compromise, poor communication, organizational dry rot, poor leadership, bad decisions, and many more.

While all ministries face many problems, not all know how to resolve those problems. A simple process that can lead to effective problem solving is threefold.

First, those directly involved with the problem need to meet together to discuss and agree on the exact nature of the problem. They need to ask, Exactly what is the problem? In some situations the answer will be evident; in others it might not be as obvious. An example of the former is a leaky roof over the church's sanctuary. An example of the latter is a recent decline in the church's attendance and giving.

Second, they need to conduct a problem analysis. This involves collecting data and opinions regarding the nature of the problem. It also involves some research and study if the problem is extremely complicated and difficult. A church's decline in attendance might be such a problem.

Finally, the team or individuals involved need to generate some alternative solutions. Often the temptation is to jump at the first available solution without considering other possible solutions. Few problems have only one solution. Involving in the process all who associate with the problem will help prevent this.

A major factor in finding the correct solution is the organization's values. The team should ask several values questions. How do our core values address this problem? What solutions do our priority values dictate or suggest, if any? Does the proposed solution contradict any of our vital values?

Problems were not strangers in the early church. Immediately the church faced the problem of selecting someone to replace Judas as a witness to the resurrection of Christ (Acts 1:21–23). Another problem was the care of believers who had physical needs (2:45). A third was the oversight of the Grecian Jews' widows in the daily distribution of food (6:1).

Regardless of the nature of the problem, the church pursued the solution based on its key values. In the replacement problem in Acts 1, the church prayed about the solution. They proposed two men and asked God to show them who was the apostolic replacement (1:23–25). Prayer was a key value and vital part of the process that led to the solution. The early church recognized that they had to address and meet people's physical needs if they were to minister to their spiritual needs. They valued the people in need more than the ownership of possessions (2:44–45; 4:34–35). Though the Twelve valued prayer and the ministry of the Word over serving the Grecian widows, they valued the women and their needs and took the necessary steps to resolve the problem (6:2–6).

PRIORITIES DETERMINATION

Every ministry has its priorities. The priorities are important because they signal not just what is important, but what is most important to an organization. In weak institutions the priorities are unclear. This may be the result of a conflict in priorities, or it could signal a tired, dying organization.

Good organizations can identify their priorities because they understand their values. Their values directly affect their priorities. However, even the ministry with a clearly articulated set of limited core values will hold some as more important than others. An understanding of the priority values is important because these values signal to the organization's followers or workers what is most important and enable them to focus their energy accordingly.

Several ways exist to discover which values in a set are high priority. Some organizations list their values in order of priority. Thus the higher-priority values are the first few on the statement. You may discover the higher-priority values in other organizations by observing what the ministry does best or where it focuses its energies.

RISK TAKING

Every Christian organization, regardless of its particular ministry, has to take risks. If it has to make decisions, then it has to take some risks. Barnabas and Paul understood this for they were "men who have risked their lives for the name of our Lord Jesus Christ" (Acts 15:26). Organizations can be found somewhere on the risk-taking continuum below, between risk resistant on one extreme and risk seeking on the other.

Risk-Taking Continuum

+————————————————————————+

Risk resistant   Risk seeking

Where a particular organization lands on the risk-taking continuum is usually up to the senior leadership, the president or leader of a parachurch ministry, or the board or pastor of a church. Most Christian institutions, especially churches, locate on the risk-resistant side. The more successful ministries in terms of vision accomplishment tend to locate more on the risk-seeking side.

The difference is the organization's quintessential values. Ministries that assign a high priority to the values of creativity and innovation are risk seeking. Those who assign them low priority or do not value them at all are at the risk-resistant extreme. The former group walks the tightrope between reasonable and excessive risk taking. The result is that they experience some big wins but may hazard some big losses. The risk-resistant group walks the line between some to very little risk taking. They are unlikely to experience significant change, and they produce little if any growth.

Values Drive the Ministry

Values Affect

▼

Decision Making
Direction and Goal Setting
Conflict Resolution
Ministry Satisfaction
Ministry Commitment
Problem Solving
Priorities Determination

The essential values of a ministry will impact more than the eight areas just mentioned. They deeply affect other areas as well, such as roles clarification; team building; monitoring, evaluation, rewards, and recognition of workers; financial management; and resource utilization. Virtually no area of ministry is exempt from the impact of the ministry's values.

Identification of Values

Sometimes it is difficult to identify a value even when using the working definition above: a constant, passionate, sacred core belief that drives the ministry. You look at a concept and it seems to fit, but you are not sure. You also realize that simply because you value something does not mean that it is a value. Therefore I offer three other distinctives of values.

Functions, Not Forms

First, we must be careful to determine the value itself, not the form it will take. The form is the means by which the value is realized. For example, some ministries such as churches list small groups as a value.

Actually the small group meeting is not the value but the form that the value may take. The real value behind many contemporary small-group programs is authentic biblical community.

To dwell on the value's form may mean missing the essence of the value altogether. For example, the small group meeting can be used to realize a number of different values. Some organizations use them for evangelism, some for pastoral care, and some for fellowship. Others use them for teaching, worship, and biblical community. Still others depend on them to accomplish all of the above. To substitute the form for the value is to miss the actual value and create some ambiguity as to the exact nature of the value.

Ends, Not Means to Ends

A second way to identify a value is to ask, Is the concept in question an end in itself or is it a means to an end? If the activity or idea is an end in itself, it is a core or essential value. If it is a means to accomplish something else, it is not the core value. Let us return to the example I used above. Is a small-group meeting an end or is it the means to an end? Meeting in a small group is not an end in itself; meeting in a group is a means to an end. Find the end and you have the value. Another example is evangelism. Basically, evangelism is a value, an end in itself, not a means to an end. We often speak of doing evangelism. In this context it may sound like the means to an end, but to do evangelism is to realize a value. A home Bible study, knocking on doors, developing a relationship—all are means to accomplish evangelism. The same is true of worship. When we go to church, we usually worship. Worship is an end in itself. To worship is to realize or experience an important biblical value. The means to that end may be singing, listening to someone else sing, reading Scripture, or hearing a message.

The Explanation for What We Do

Another way to discern the value is by asking the why question, *Why* do we do what we do? The reason you do something, not *what* you are doing, identifies the essential value. Gathering together in a group is not as important as the reason you are gathered. Gathering in a group is the what; the reason you gather is the why. The *what* is the form that the value takes; the *why* identifies the value itself. A group of Christians may decide to go out and knock on doors one Saturday afternoon. That is not a value. The answer to the question, Why are you knocking on doors? identifies the core value. The answer may reflect on the people behind those doors—to see them come to faith in Christ (evangelism). The answer could also involve the people who are knocking. They may argue that they are knocking on doors for evangelism, but the real reason is to spend some time together (fellowship).

Kinds of Values

In defining core values, it has been helpful to consider what they are not as well as what they are. We can further hone and refine the definition by examining different kinds of values. There are six kinds of values that exist in tension.

Conscious versus Unconscious Values

The core organizational beliefs of all Christian ministries exist at both a conscious and an unconscious level. To some degree those involved in the ministry are aware of the values that are most important and of high priority. An evangelistic organization is well aware that it values evangelism; a school or seminary knows that it values teaching. Most ministries, however, hold the majority of their values at a subconscious level. This is because they have numerous values, and even though these values influence decisions made every day, the ministry participants have not actually stopped to think about or discuss most of them.

Leaders are responsible for discovering and articulating the institution's primary values. When values are articulated—conscious—leaders know why they are doing what they are doing. If they hold some bad values or some that their ministry's constituency does not share, they will be aware of them and can make changes accordingly. If people in the ministry have sharp disagreements with one another, they will know how to find solutions because they have identified their key values.

Leaders who hold their beliefs at a conscious level tend to be proactive. They are initiators who have thought through what they are doing. They know what they believe and why they believe it, and those values drive them. Reactive leaders often hold their values at an unconscious level. They tend to be driven not so much by their values as by their moods, the weather, and other external factors. Stephen Covey writes, "The ability to subordinate an impulse to a value is the essence of the proactive person. Reactive people are driven by feelings, by circumstances, by conditions, by their environment. Proactive people are driven by values—carefully thought about, selected, and internalized values."[18]

Leaders and the members of their organizations hold a significant number of different values, probably in the hundreds. But they are not aware of them because they hold the majority at the unconscious level. Leaders must know their high-priority organizational values and hold them at the conscious level. The lower-priority beliefs may remain at an unconscious level.

Luke articulates the core values of the Jerusalem church in Acts 2:42–47. They consist of the apostles' teaching, the fellowship, the breaking of bread, prayer, the sharing of possessions, and praise. Clearly, the church was aware of its essential, high-priority values. No one debates that this church and its leaders were proactive, as evidenced by its evangelism thrust (2:41, 47; 4:4) and the ministries of Peter and others recorded in the early chapters of Acts.

Shared versus Unshared Values

In their book *In Search of Excellence,* Tom Peters and Robert Waterman write: "I believe the real difference between success and failure in a corporation can very often be traced to the question of how well the organization brings out the great energies and talents of its people. What does it do to help these people find common cause with each other?"[19] I believe that they are correct, and although they use the term *corporation,* this would apply to all Christian organizations as well. Shared values become the common cause that is so vital to realizing a ministry's vision. If the lay or professional followers in a ministry share the same values as the leadership, together they will accomplish their mission.

Shared values benefit an organization in a number of ways. Kouzes and Posner conducted research that involved more than twenty-three hundred managers at all levels, representing public and private organizations located across the United States, regarding the importance of shared values. These studies revealed that shared values:

- foster strong feelings of personal effectiveness
- promote high levels of company loyalty
- facilitate consensus about key organization goals and stakeholders
- encourage ethical behavior
- promote strong norms about working hard and caring
- reduce levels of job stress and tension[20]

Although Kouzes and Posner do not comment on the nature of the surveyed organizations, whether or not any are Christian, there is no reason why Christian organizations should not share these benefits. Believers in an organization who share the same values feel a deep sense of effectiveness, are intensely loyal, agree on key ministry goals, behave ethically, work hard, care deeply, and experience less stress and tension on the job.

Shared values deeply affect the ministry's vision. They serve to garner the needed enthusiasm and support that is vital for the success of the vision. They also have a coalescing effect. They serve to unite the professional staff and any volunteer staff to realize God's vision for the ministry. Shared values help to both identify and then overcome vision obstacles. Any obstacles to the ministry dream most often lie in the area of disparate values. If any leaders or groups in the organization are resistant to the vision, look for foundational differences in the area of their values.

Shared values also serve as a channel to direct the tremendous energy that is resident in the organization and its people. Every Christian organization has a great amount of energy available to it. This energy resides in the people who make up the ministry and increases proportionately with how much these people enjoy their work, share common cause, and walk in the Spirit. Shared values contribute to their enjoyment of the ministry and help them know where to focus their energy. In ministries where people do not share the values, less energy exists, and that energy quickly dissipates because it moves in many different directions at the same time.

A common characteristic of strong, godly churches is shared, biblical corporate values. The people who make up these churches share the same values and are pulling in the same direction. In Acts 4:32 Luke indicates that the Jerusalem church held common beliefs: "All the believers were one in heart and mind." And we see the impact on their lives: "No one claimed that any of his possessions was his own, but they shared everything they had."

Churches that do not share the same values are splits waiting to happen. Paul wrote the first six chapters of 1 Corinthians as an attempt to correct the serious divisions that existed among the Corinthian people, which rested ultimately on their values (1 Cor. 1:10–17). A ministry cannot survive without a consensus on values. Eventually some people will have to give in or leave.

Some research shows that bringing people with different values into an organization can be good for a struggling ministry. The reason is that it slows or even reverses inertia and allows the organization to take advantage of new opportunities.[21] Thus a dying congregation could benefit by bringing in a pastor with different values who would attract people with different values. At the same time, the congregation must be open to and willing to accept new ideas and ways of doing ministry. Some can do this; most struggle with such changes. The same research shows that people with an extremely low (negative) fit will bring dissent and may even attempt to sabotage the organization. Once they become members, they will try to change the ministry's values through personal control and power so that those values match their own.[22]

Personal versus Organizational Values

A person's organizational values resemble a ministry's organizational values. Both concern the ministry organization. One difference between them, however, is that the latter values affect all who make up the organization, whereas personal values affect primarily the individual but have the potential to affect the entire organization.

Every institution has a core set of organizational values. We have seen the importance of these key values in driving the organization. (I refer to these as *organizational, institutional,* or *corporate values*. They are valid terms to use in describing a sacred or a secular institution. When referring specifically to a Christian organization, I often use the term *ministry,* and if it is a church, I may use the adjective *congregational*.) Individuals who make up the institution also have a set of core values. (I call them *personal, individual,* or *private organizational values*.) These are values that concern the organization as a whole. Every person brings to a ministry his or her own private set of core beliefs about what should drive that ministry.

Like the organizational values, individual values can be helpful or harmful. This is why it is so important that people bring to the surface the general values for ministry organizations, such as the church, that they have acquired over the years. They should ask such questions as, Are my values for this ministry going to help or harm it? Are they reasonable or unreasonable? Do my values agree with those of the ministry of which I am a part?

The latter question raises again the issue of shared values. One reason it is so important to discover and be aware of both individual and corporate values is to see if they are shared. A Christian should not work for any organization, sacred or secular, if he or she does not share to a great degree the institutional values. A person should not join a church if he or she does not share its values. A pastor should not take a church, nor should a church hire a pastor, if the church and pastor do not have consensus on the ministry's key values. The same is true for two churches that are considering a merger. They should not do so unless there is substantial agreement on their core ideals. To settle for less in any of these situations is to court spiritual and emotional disaster.

Actual versus Aspirational Values

Leaders and organizations have both actual and aspirational core values. Actual values are the beliefs they own and act on daily. These values come from inside the person. They exist in the present and they have to do with what is true about the ministry right now. Aspirational values are beliefs that the individual or organization does not currently own. They deal with what should or ought to be, not with what is; they may be values that the leadership or organization would like to adopt in the future. Until they are adopted, however, they remain aspirational. A number of churches today are not very evangelistic. Consequently, for them to list evangelism as an actual value is a mistake. They should view it as an aspirational value.

Most of this book focuses on actual not aspirational values. The key to understanding what drives you or your ministry is not what you would like to value as much as what you do value. You cannot fake your values or your vision. Nor can you intellectualize or rationalize them. You must passionately hold your core values, as well as your vision, at a gut level right now, today.

Your core values or beliefs are a part of you. Thus as a leader you impart your personal values for the ministry through your daily actions. And this is why it is so important that you deal with real not aspirational values. You do not establish values as much as you operate on existing values. The immediate question is not, What values or beliefs should we adopt? The important question is, What values or beliefs have we adopted? Operating from the former is inauthentic; operating from the latter is authentic. An exception to this would involve letting people know that some values are actual while others are aspirational. You could state this either in the value statement itself or in the introduction to the entire credo. Another approach is to put an asterisk after the aspirational values. Regardless, people involved in a ministry know what values are actual or aspirational. If you claim the latter as the former, they will question your honesty.

The core values of the Jerusalem church, as found in Acts 2:42–47, are actual not aspirational values. The difference is at the beginning of verse 42: "They devoted themselves to the apostles' teaching . . . the fellowship . . . the breaking of bread . . . prayer." The very fact that the church was deeply immersed in these four spiritual activities marks the activities as real values. If the text said that they discussed them or debated the need to pursue them, they would be aspirational values.

You may be a leader or the new pastor of an older church that is plateaued or dying. It will not take you long to realize that the church needs to grow and to reach a younger generation if it is to survive. An important first step is for you to unearth the church's controlling organizational values. If, in developing a values credo, you include evangelism as a core value of the church, you would be mistaken. If the church is not involved in evangelism, evangelism cannot be a core value. It may be an aspirational value, however. By discovering the church's real values, you will gain much insight into its crippling problems.

An important part of your job as a leader is to take the next step as well. Eventually you will need to think about aspirational values. You should ask, What should be this church's values? What key value ingredients are missing in the church's ministry menu? And most important, Can I lead this church to adopt a new set of biblical values? You should be aware that the latter is a very difficult, painful process. Most churches that are in trouble will resist what they need most—a complete or partial transition from one set of values to another.

Single versus Multiple Values

All organizations have multiple values. In larger corporations with numerous people, there can be hundreds of values. An organization's core values, however, are those that are the highest in priority, and in some institutions, a single, overriding core value exists. If you listed the values in order of priority, you would find it at the top of the list, often with some distance between it and the rest. It's like an umbrella with the other values appropriately arranged under it.

In a congregational context, a single robust value often serves to unify the church and communicates the church's central thrust. It announces what the church is all about, what it stands for. The following chart presents several North American church paradigms and the unifying, dominating core value of each. We will look at the first paradigm to get an idea of what the chart is communicating about each value.

The first is the classroom church. The overriding or unifying value is information or Bible doctrine. That is what is distinctive about this ministry. It communicates that if you want to know the Bible, this is the church for you. You can see how this one potent value affects all the ministry. It clearly defines the role of the pastor and the people. It sets the key emphasis (to know) in concrete. And it dictates the desired result (an educated Christian).

An organization or church ministry would be wise to examine its essential beliefs to determine if it has a unifying or overarching value. Many do. However, this unifying value may or may not be desirable, depending on the ministry's vision and purpose. When my church-planting students at Dallas Seminary examine this chart, they view it through Great Commission eyes. The result for them is that most of the churches with a single, unifying value prove inadequate because they emphasize some aspect of the Great Commission and not the commission as a whole. Thus they specialize, more like a parachurch ministry than a church ministry.

This chart also demonstrates the power of a value in the life of a church. For example, the value dictates congregational expectations for the pastor and the pastor's expectations of the people. The same holds for the church's purpose, typical tool, and desired results.

The Power of a Value

American Evangelical Churches

Type of Church	Unifying Value	Role of Pastor	Role of People	Primary Purpose	Typical Tool	Desired Result
Classroom church	Doctrine	Teacher	Students	To know	Sermon outline	Educated Christians
Soul-winning church	Evangelism	Evangelist	Bringers	To save	Altar call	Born-again persons
Experiential church	Worship	Worship leader	Worshipers	To exalt	Handheld mike	Committed Christians
Family-reunion church	Fellowship	Chaplain	Siblings	To belong	Potluck	Secure Christians

Congruent versus Incongruent Values

A principal reason some Christian organizations have reached their goals while others have not is congruent core values. These are the beliefs that serve the ministry well because they, like the pieces of a puzzle, fit together and, like close family members, support one another. When the corporation lists and articulates its essential values, congruent beliefs hang together or align with one another.

Incongruent values affect a ministry in much the same way as mixing together the pieces of two separate puzzles affects the novice who, unaware of what has happened, attempts to put them together. Incongruent values are in conflict. The result is ministry chaos, which leads to extreme ministry frustration. The conflicting values held by members of such ministries dissipate much of the creative energy and leave little room for constructive ministry. The ministry participants are often at one another's throats, emotionally and sometimes physically. One former student, for example, who became a pastor, told me of the head deacon in his first church. The man could not control his temper and would challenge those who disagreed with him to a fistfight right in the middle of a board meeting.

Two potentially incongruent values for some churches are valuing the poor while maintaining a high-quality facility. Most congregations find that the two don't mix. However, Harold Westing, in his book *Create and Celebrate Your Church's Uniqueness,* gives an unusual example of how these seemingly incongruent values are congruent congregational values at First Assembly Church in Phoenix, Arizona.

They have an outstanding ministry to the poor. They go into the inner city to minister, and they bring inner-city dwellers to their very attractive facility in the suburbs of the city. Two values are tied together there. "We want these poor people to be treated with respect," Tommy Barnett said. "So we want them to be in a beautiful setting." First Assembly places a high value on having the most attractive facility possible, while at the same time giving as much help to the poor as they possibly can.[23]

Numerous examples of incongruent values exist. A Christian company hires and rewards its employees based on their ability to be creative and innovative in their work, while leaving in key positions some trusted old-timers who insist on the tried and true. A church may value evangelism but use irrelevant, outdated methods in its attempt to reach today's lost unchurched. Unlike First Assembly of Phoenix, a congregation may have a thriving ministry to the poor and oppressed in the inner city but would never invite them to their attractive facilities in the suburbs. A church may allow only traditional worship in its services but be willing to plant a church that worships with a contemporary style. A board may create all kinds of programs for its younger adults and their children but never allow them to sit in any important leadership positions. While all these values may be good in themselves, they fail to align well with one another and serve more as a detriment than as a complement to the organization.

Kinds of Values

Conscious	Unconscious
Shared	Unshared
Personal	Organizational
Actual	Aspirational
Single	Multiple
Congruent	Incongruent

Questions for Reflection and Discussion

1. What are some differences between a church's core values and its vision and strategy? What is the difference between a key value and a vision?

2. Why is it so important that a church have constant values? Does this mean that it should never change its values? Under what circumstances might they change? How much should they change?

3. Why is it so important that you have passionate values? What should you do if your primary values are not passionate?

4. Why is it so important that your values be sacred? Are traditions based on biblical values? What should you do if they are not biblical?

5. What are some ways that central beliefs drive a church's ministry? How much importance would you attach to each? What are some other ways that beliefs drive a ministry?

6. What values does your ministry hold on a conscious level? Can you identify any values that it holds on an unconscious level? How have the conscious and unconscious values affected the ministry?

7. Identify your church's shared values. Why are shared values so important? What values are not shared? How have they affected the ministry adversely?

8. What personal ministry beliefs do you share with your church? What values are not shared? Which is the greater number? How has this affected your attitude toward and involvement in your church?

9. What are some aspirational values that you desire for your church or for any ministry that you are a part of? Does your church or other ministry have a single, dominant value? If so, what is it?

10. Have you observed any values in a Christian organization (church or parachurch) that are incongruent? If so, what are they? How have they affected the ministry adversely?

3

WHAT DRIVES YOU?
THE DISCOVERY OF CORE VALUES

Whether they were aware of them or not, both Pastor David Johnson and Hope Community Church had a set of core values. The fact that they had not surfaced and been articulated proved costly to both. Many organizations have given little or no attention to the vital, shaping beliefs that drive the institution and underlie the behavior of the leaders and members. These values are ever present and are vital determinants of behavior; yet rarely do leaders consciously express them, and even more rarely do they discover and discuss them in an open fashion to determine which values are helpful or harmful to the ministry.

What if Pastor David and Hope Church had desired to discover their key organizational values? Suppose that David had returned to seminary for a continuing education class or had enrolled in a doctor of ministry program, and a skilled, knowledgeable professor had required the class to identify and develop a personal or congregational ministry credo. How would he have gone about the process? What does a leader or an organization do to unearth values? The values-discovery process consists of five elements: a decision concerning who is responsible for discovering the values, a determination of what values you will seek to discover, the reasons for discovering these values, the discovery of the church's actual values, and the establishing of its aspirational values.

Who Discovers the Core Values?

The Point Person

The first element asks, Who is involved in the values-discovery process? The general answer is, all who are in the ministry. The primary responsibility to see that it takes place is with the leadership, and in particular, with the point person in the organization. The point person is the primary leader of the organization—the leader of the leaders. In the parachurch, this person is the president, the general director, or the ministry leader. In the marketplace, this individual is the CEO or the president. In the church, the focus of this book, the point person is the senior pastor or the only pastor, such as Pastor David Johnson.

Most people in an organization look to the top for a definition of what is really important, what the ministry's bottom line is. The leader may or may not be the author of the key values, but the leader is responsible for their discovery, making them clear, and ensuring that all live up to them in the decision-making process. One of the great contributions a leader can make to a ministry is to help unearth, clarify, and breathe life into its significant beliefs. The leader, however, does not accomplish this by himself or herself but sees to it that it is accomplished.

A Ministry Team

To discover the key beliefs, it is imperative that the leader enlist the aid of other leaders or the leadership team in the ministry for their knowledge of the ministry and for their objectivity. The old leadership paradigm looks to the pastor to do all the ministry and make all the ministry decisions. The new paradigm looks to those leaders sprinkled throughout the ministry to be involved in the process. I refer to them as the church's E. F. Hutton people—from the old E. F. Hutton television commercial that stated, "When E. F. Hutton [an investment broker] speaks, people listen." In the church these E. F. Hutton people have influence no matter their ministry, position, or lack thereof. They are people on the church board, staff, pastor, and lay leaders, such as Sunday school teachers and others.

In the church, the size of the ministry usually dictates the number of persons involved. A small church may have as many as five or so people. In a larger ministry, I've worked with as many as thirty leaders, each with their circles of influence in the church. If this number seems too large, keep in mind that some will always be absent from teamwork meetings due to other responsibilities.

Finally, research tells us that for a person to really understand the values of an organization, he or she needs to have been a part of it for at least one to two years. Consequently, those new to the ministry may defer to those that have been around for two or more years.[1] On the other hand, those new to a ministry may bring needed objectivity.

What Values?

Personal Ministry Values

The values-discovery process examines both the personal and corporate values held by an organization.

Leadership Team

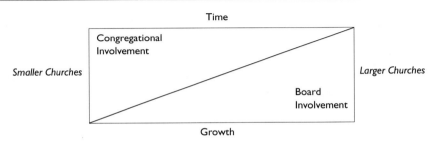

Values discovery begins at the individual or personal level. In an entrepreneurial ministry such as a church plant, the point person, especially if he or she is a lone ranger—not working with a team—must identify and cast his or her values for the ministry. Then, when others consider joining the core group, they can look for common cause to determine if there is a ministry fit. It is most important that the primary leader and the key decision makers in an established ministry be clear about their own values and recognize any differences between them.

Organizational Ministry Values

Next, values discovery moves to the ministry institution itself. This includes two levels. The first is the values set that drives the entire ministry as a whole. These values make up the ministry's credo. They communicate the distinctiveness of this ministry as well as what the entire organization is all about.

The second level is the values of the organizations or ministries that make up the broader corporation—the under-the-umbrella ministries.

In the church they may include Christian education, worship, small groups, outreach, drama, and so on. In the best of all worlds, all the under-the-umbrella ministries hold to the same values as the entire organization, but they have developed significant values that are unique to their particular ministries. For example, the church may value excellence in its ministries. It believes that whatever it does, it should be done well. The Christian education department embraces this value and attempts to recruit and use gifted teachers. After all, it only makes sense that if you have a teaching ministry, you would use those to whom God has given a teaching gift. However, a value unique to this department may be a team-teaching approach or the use of male teachers in the children's ministries.[2]

Why Discover the Values?

You will recall that chapter 1 provides ten answers to the question, Why discover the values? Here is a recap of those answers.

1. Values discovery and clarification empower a ministry to know its distinctives.
2. Values help people outside the ministry determine if it is a ministry for them. This answers the question, Do we join or look further?
3. Values communicate what is important to the organization. People know where to focus their energies.
4. Values help people embrace positive change. They determine what change will be helpful or harmful to the ministry.
5. Values influence the organization's overall behavior. They drive the decisions made, problems resolved, goals set, and so on.
6. Values inspire people to action. Common values catalyze ministry involvement.
7. Values enhance credible leadership. Leaders who act according to their professed values gain valuable credibility in the eyes of their people.
8. Clarified values shape the ministry's character—they are character defining. They affect how the organization conducts its ministry.
9. Values contribute to the ministry's success in that they generate deeper personal involvement in the life of its employees or members.
10. Values determine the ministry's vision. They are the hidden motivators that guide the selection of the vision.

Other reasons exist besides these ten. Another primary one is the biblical example in Acts 2:42–47. The Jerusalem church had a set of core values, they knew these values, and they lived by them to the point that observers could even articulate them. Luke, the writer of Acts, not only lists these values for us, but in Acts 2:42, he writes: "They devoted themselves to . . ." Their values were evident in their actions. People could see what the church was devoted to by what they did. Their actions evidenced their values. Obviously the church knew the things they were doing because they did them together as a faith community. As I will show later, they used these values in a values-resolution process. If the early church knew and operated on their values, wisdom dictates that today's churches should follow suit.

Another reason to identify core values is that when ministries know and are explicit about their core values, they can legitimately expect people to abide by them. Let us assume that Hope Church had discovered their legitimate core values and had written them in a church credo, which they presented to David Johnson during the engagement period. If he had taken the pastoral position knowing these beliefs, he would have been responsible for directing the ministry accordingly. However, had he accepted the pastorate knowing that he differed fundamentally with the church's statement of values, he would have violated his integrity. I also believe that he could have violated ethics had he taken the position knowing that he differed but hoping to lead the church to adopt other values—namely, his own. The same would have been true of Hope Church had they married David while knowing that he held to different core beliefs.

This applies to all the people who joined Hope Community Church after they had written their church credo. Had the church clearly communicated its values to them, people would have been wrong to join the church in hopes of changing it. Since no perfect church exists, everyone who joins a church will not find, nor should he or she expect to find, total values agreement. People join by consensus; that is, they agree to disagree on some values. However, once they decide to join, they must realize that the church does not owe it to them to adopt their differing values. It is unfair to any organization for you to join it, knowing that you differ, and then to conduct a major campaign to change it.

Ministries should know what they truly believe and then capitalize on it, so long as it does not violate Scripture. They should resist the temptation to adopt wholesale the values of other more successful ministries. In North America 80 to 85 percent or more of the church and parachurch ministries are plateaued or in decline. Often the leaders, pastors, and boards of these organizations look at the 15 percent that are growing to determine what changes they should make in their own ministries. For example, Willow Creek Community Church has a large, thriving ministry northwest of Chicago. They hold three pastors' conferences every year. Unfortunately, pastors and lay leaders leave those conferences convinced that they must change their churches to be like Willow Creek, in spite of warnings to the contrary.

The problem is that these pastors and lay leaders are attempting to move from their actual values to embrace aspirational values. This is a difficult, time-consuming process. Most churches will not survive it. These churches would be better off to discover their own values and to emphasize their strong biblical beliefs while seeking to rid themselves of harmful values. Most often it is the latter, not the former, that are the problem. The solution lies not in mimicking others but in capitalizing on the good values that already exist.

Discovering Ministry Values

How are the values discovered? I will suggest a number of ways, but first we must consider some introductory matters. Values discovery attempts to determine why an individual or organization does what it does. In this process, it is important to remember that people are not creating or shaping their primary values; they are discovering them. They are attempting to bring to the surface actual, not aspirational, beliefs. The process has to be authentic; they cannot fake core values, nor can they intellectualize them. People unearth their values by looking inside. They must hold these values passionately at a gut level or else they are not core. In effect they are taking these values out, dusting them off, and taking a hard look at what they already own, not at what they plan to adopt in the future.

Since organizational values exist on both the personal and the corporate level, the leadership should seek to detect their values at both levels. Discovery should begin at the personal level with those who are the leaders and key decision makers in the organization—the ministry team. Most likely they are the ones who will unearth the ministry's values. They need to be clear about their own personal credos and any differences they may have with other leaders and decision makers as well as with the church.

Personal Ministry Values

Several techniques exist for discovering the actual values on the individual level. As you apply any such techniques, ask, What is the evidence that I hold this as an actual value?

Write out your values. Ask each person to write out his or her beliefs. Some preparation for this assignment is necessary. You must define or explain what a core value is. I suggest that you use the working definition in chapter 2. It might be helpful to expose the individuals to several sample credos, such as those found in the appendixes. If they are attempting to discover their organizational beliefs for a church, take them to appendix A; for a parachurch ministry, show them appendix B; for the marketplace, go to appendix C. Make sure this exposure is brief, because you do not want the sample values to unduly influence the participants. When each person has written down an exhaustive list, ask him or her to prioritize those values. Often the first two or three values are priorities because the most important ones tend to surface first. I call this the "cold turkey" approach, because people come to the values-discovery process cold—without much knowledge of what they are doing. Thus I would advise that you not rely on this technique alone.

Take a values audit. Another technique is to take a values audit such as the Personal Ministry Core Values Audit located in appendix D. I designed this audit primarily for the church, but it may be applicable to the parachurch, since it represents a good cross section of the beliefs found in most church or parachurch ministries. Ask the individuals to look over the list and mark those that they believe are their actual (not aspirational) ministry core values. As they work through the list, some values will stand out as clear, felt values and some will not. Each individual may add values that are not on the list, in the space provided at the end. The person should rate them on a scale from 1, the lowest, to 5, the highest value. At the end, he or she is to write down all those rated as a 4 or 5 and prioritize them by placing a 1 in front of the highest, and so on.

Study others' value statements. A third technique is to focus on the credos in the appendixes of this book. The idea is to concentrate on them and to study them in much more detail than in the first technique. As a person works through them, he or she should list those that stand out, much as in the second technique above. The question people are to answer is not, What values *should* you hold? but, What values *do* you hold? What values attract your attention? Most often people are drawn to the values or beliefs they share. This has to do with the passions that tap a person's emotions. Because you identify with them emotionally, they tend to jump off the page at you. I suggest that those involved in vocational ministry begin to collect their own set of credos from various ministries and add them to the ones in the appendixes for present and later use. I suspect that their experience will be much like mine. They will find that few churches have credos, but over a period of several years, they will be able to gather a small number.

Describe the ideal church. A fourth technique is to ask each person who desires to know his or her personal values for the organization to write a description of the ideal ministry of the type he or she is involved in. For a church this would include such things as what takes place on Sunday mornings and evenings as well as during the week. He or she could describe the ideal pastor, staff, and congregation and discuss how the church is run. This exercise will cause a number of values to surface, such as the kind of worship (traditional or contemporary), the importance of Scripture and expository preaching, the relevance of small groups and attempts to experience biblical community, the position and role of the pastor and staff, and so on.

Corporate Ministry Values

Several techniques exist for discovering values on the organizational level. They will help you discover the values of an organization you may want to join or may already be a part of, such as a church or a parachurch ministry; they will also unearth the beliefs of a ministry you may want to work for or volunteer to serve. As the ministry team works through these techniques, again ask, What is the evidence that we hold and practice these values? (Scholars note that it takes around a year of involvement in the organization to really get to know its values.)

Request the church's credo. One technique is to ask for a copy of the ministry's statement of values. Do not be surprised, however, if they do not have a credo or even know what you are talking about since this concept is so new.

Articulate observed values. A second technique is to write down what you believe the institution's values are. This technique requires that you have some involvement in the organization over time. When you attend the meetings of a church or parachurch ministry for a while, you should be able to discern their core values based on what they do or do not do, their emphases, or where they spend money. Had you lived in Jerusalem in the first century, you would have easily discovered the Jerusalem church's credo through observation, for, as noted earlier, Luke tells us, "They devoted themselves to . . ." Their actions evidenced their values; they fleshed them out in their lives.

Do a congregational values audit. A third technique is to complete the Church Ministry Core Values Audit located in appendix D. I have designed this audit to help people discover the beliefs of a church of which they are a part or of which they may become a part. If you have moved to a new area or if you are changing churches, you could use some of the items in this audit as interview questions for the staff or laypeople who are a part of the church you are considering. Several other audits are available. Milton Rokeach has developed the Rokeach Value Survey that has become the standard for many.[3] Another is a values questionnaire by

Paul McDonald and Jeffrey Gandz.[4] The problem, however, with these and other similar values questionnaires is that they are primarily for the marketplace and not the ministry world. Hence, they do not include such values as evangelism, worship, fellowship, and the like.

Request a copy of the church's budget. A fourth technique is to analyze the ministry's budget. Like people, churches spend money on what they value most. Consequently, you will likely gain insight into a ministry's values by requesting a copy of the budget. For example, if the church sets aside funds for evangelism ministries, it likely holds evangelism as an actual core value.

Conduct a storyboard session. The storyboard process is the primary technique that I use as a consultant to help a leadership team discover its church's core values. It combines a values audit with brainstorming and a critical thinking process. I have the leadership team take the church core values audit (appendix D). Then I ask them to articulate what they think the ministry's core values are, based on that audit. I write these on yellow 3" x 5" cards and pin them to a flannel board. Finally, in an effort to narrow down the number of core values, I give six red dots per person to the team members and ask them to stick one dot on a core they believe is basic to their church. We can know the ministry's values by noting which cards have the most dots. I describe this process more in depth in chapter 1 of my book *Advanced Strategic Planning* (Baker).

Storyboarding is also known as compression planning. It can be used for other purposes as well as for strategic planning. I cannot say enough good things about this technique and would highly recommend it to any ministry that wants to plan well and save time in the process.

Regardless of how we unearth an organization's values or our personal ministry values, we should in either case limit the total number to six, because we are not after just any values but the core values. This is why it is important to list personal values and ministry values in order of priority. I will say more about this in my discussion of aspirational values at the end of this chapter.

The Benefit of Knowing Core Values

Earlier in this book, I stated that one of the biggest reasons people leave a ministry is that they do not share enough core values. This was a major reason why the marriage of Pastor David Johnson and Hope Church ended in divorce. I argue that had both David Johnson and Hope Church taken time to identify their values and look for common cause, they would never have entered into the marriage.

But this raises the all-important question, How could they have known that they did not share mutual values before the marriage? The common problem is the engagement period. In most church contexts, it is too short. When a pastor leaves, the church appoints either the board or a pulpit committee, representing the different interests in the church, to search for and locate a new pastor. The typical, inexperienced board meets and quickly decides that they are not going to rush into this process: "No need to get in any big hurry—we'd pick the wrong person for sure!" Ten months later, someone notes that attendance is way down, and the treasurer informs the board that if something does not change drastically, the church will be out of business in just a few months.

Armed with this information, the board or pulpit committee springs into action, and within a month or two a promising candidate shows up on Sunday, and the church votes him in the following week. And that is the problem. The preengagement involves looking over a number of résumés and phoning the references of the best candidates. The typical engagement period consists of a weekend or weeklong visit during which the candidate preaches on Sunday morning and evening and visits with the board or pulpit committee. If he makes all the right moves, the church will vote him in. Neither the candidate nor the church can know in such a short period if they share common cause.

The solution to this problem for the candidate is to request a copy of the church's credo (if it has one) and its budget or ask it to complete the Church Ministry Core Values Audit. A solution for the church is to ask the prospective pastor to complete the Personal Ministry Core Values Audit.

It's a good idea for the candidate and the church to use these resources before the candidate visits the church. This could save them the time and expense of a trip, or it could result in a more profitable trip in the kinds of issues they address during the brief time they are together.

The Test of a Good Value

As you discover your values, how can you know if they are good ones? Remember, according to the definition in chapter 2, a good value meets at least five criteria: It is constant, passionate, sacred, a belief, and it drives or directs the ministry.

A Good Core Value Is Constant

Will this value stand the test of time? More important, will people strive to live for this value two, five, ten, twenty-five years from now?

In a time of accelerating, cataclysmic change, core beliefs must remain intact in a visionary ministry, or the ministry will quickly plateau and begin to decline. Do you plan to hold this value as core no matter how the world around you changes? Would it be up for grabs if the world in general, or the ministry world in particular, ceased to reward you or even went so far as to penalize you for holding this value, as happened to the early church in the context of a pagan Roman culture?

A Good Core Value Is Passionate

Does this value touch people's emotions? Passion is a feeling word. It is what you feel strongly and care deeply about. Thus it is associated with the emotions. At the same time, it does not exclude the intellect. If people are passionate about a value, they must think about it too. The value moves through the brain on the way to the heart. When it reaches the heart, it prods the emotions. It stirs something inside so that it is not soon forgotten.

A value should do more than stir the emotions and stick in the memory, however. It must also be inspirational; it must move people to action. It will not sit idly on some shelf; it refuses to quietly fill a file. Instead, in some way, big or small, it affects the decisions the members make and the relationships that take place within the organization.

A Good Core Value Is Sacred

As we saw in Acts 2:42–47, the Jerusalem church had a set of biblical core values. We should be able to find a good core value in the Bible, or it should at least agree with the Scriptures. All of a ministry's values must find their source in Scripture or not differ from it. The fact that you cannot initially find biblical support does not mean that it does not exist. You may need to give it some time and to ask other biblically knowledgeable people for their opinions. For example, some leaders value creativity and innovation in their ministries. They want to find and implement new ideas, strategies, and methods, and they appreciate adaptability and flexibility. The Bible supports this value in Genesis 1 and 2. God is a creative God, and he is engaged in the creative process in these two chapters that record his creation of the world. If you can find no biblical support for a certain value and have consulted with other knowledgeable people, eventually you should question whether it agrees with Scripture. While it is not imperative that you support every value with a biblical text, values must be sacred and must not contradict the Bible.

A Good Core Value Is a Belief

A test of values focuses on your beliefs. Values are rooted in your core or central beliefs. But what is a belief? We learned in chapter 2 that a *belief* is a conviction or opinion that you hold to be true based on limited evidence or proof. It is something that you trust or have faith in. Thus, by definition, a belief is not a fact. A fact is a conviction that a significant number of people hold to be true, based on fairly extensive evidence. The difference is in the number of people who hold a conviction and the amount of evidence that authenticates the conviction.

Make sure that what you call a value is a belief and not something else, such as a doctrine, a vision, or your strategy (see chapter 2).

A Good Core Value Drives the Ministry

The organization's central values are the beliefs that direct the ministry. In chapter 2, I compared them to the driver sitting behind the wheel of the ministry car. While a ministry is vision focused, it is values driven. Values shape the ministry, guiding most of what it does and how it does it. They direct all that the ministry seeks to accomplish and define everyone's job. Values represent the bottom line for what the church will and will not do—the deeply ingrained influencers behind all of its behavior, including many vital areas, such as decision making, direction and goal setting, conflict resolution, ministry satisfaction, ministry commitment, problem solving, priorities determination, and risk taking. If your so-called core values do not direct the ministry, then they are aspirational values. That means that you need to revisit and repeat the values-discovery process. Something went wrong, and you have not yet identified your actual ministry values.

The Test of a Good Value

- Is it constant?
- Does it engender passion?
- Is it sacred?
- Is it a belief?
- Does it drive the ministry?

Comparing and Communicating the Results

After people have completed the values-discovery process, they should compare and communicate the results. The initial result of the process for an individual such as David Johnson is that he knows his essential core values, both good and bad. The same is true for an organization like Hope Community Church. Where comparison and communication are especially helpful is in showing how the individual's results relate to others in the organization, such as the staff, and to the entire organization.

The Senior Pastor and the Staff

David Johnson could become the senior pastor of a church with two or more people on staff. If all go through the discovery process, they need to compare the results to discover common cause. The intersecting circles in the following graphs serve well in communicating the results. Each circle represents a staff person, and where the circles overlap (shaded areas), they have common cause. The greater the shaded area, the more they share common cause. The team in the figure on the left has less in common than the one in the figure on the right, and the chances of the first team working well together are not as good as those of the other team. Thus a critical factor in hiring staff is values congruence.

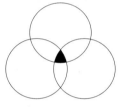 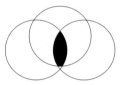

Less in common   More in common

The Senior Pastor and the Church

Another approach is to compare candidate David Johnson's values results with those of Hope Church. Let us assume that David discovers that he has five core values, and the church also has five. However, they hold only two values in common. If they divide ten, the total number of values, by the two common values, they have approximately 20 percent common cause. The first bar graph below communicates this result. Unless they can come to some kind of agreement, which is not likely, this is not a good fit for either of them.

However, the discovery process might reveal that they agree on seven values. That would mean that they have 70 percent agreement, as shown in the next bar graph. Except for a few unusual ministry circumstances, agreement on at least 50 to 60 percent of the core precepts is necessary for a good marriage.[5] The higher the percentage, the better the marriage.

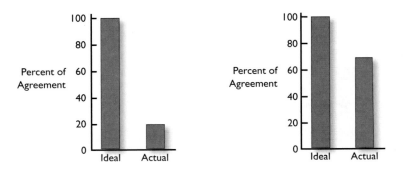

Some Options for Values Misalignments

What are some of the options that a person has if his or her values do not align with those of the ministry?

Change your values. One option is for a person to change his or her personal ministry values. Chatman notes that this works when the organization's values are stronger than the person's and the person is open to such influence.[6] An individual's personal ministry values are shaped by the values of the church that led him or her to faith (especially at an older age) as well as by the values of the church that helped the person make a full commitment to the lordship of Christ. When these experiences have influenced a person's values, it is unlikely that he or she will change these values to conform to those of a ministry. However, Chatman found that people will change and adopt the values that were rewarded in previous organizations or occupations.[7] Weiss found that people aligned their values with those of the leaders they perceived to be considerate, competent, and successful.[8]

Change the organization's values. Another option is changing the church's ministry values. Chatman says there is evidence to suggest that people can bring about change in their organization.[9] My experience has been that a leader, such as a senior pastor, can effect a values change in a church, but it usually takes time, and far too many pastors do not wait around long enough to see this happen. Kohn and Schooler found that people influenced their jobs more than their jobs influenced them.[10] Chatman observes that when an individual enters an organization with deep-seated values and the individual is strong on personal control and self-efficacy, or when many members join at once who share the same values, the organization will become more like the individuals over time.[11] As noted earlier, some research shows that bringing in people with different values can be good for the struggling organization—it slows or reverses inertia and allows the people to take advantage of new opportunities. This could happen to a dying church with a new pastor whose values differ from those of the church. However, extremely low (negative) fit may result in sabotage or dissent rather than in a positive effect.[12]

Abandon the church. A third option is to leave the organization. Chatman observes that this happens more often when an organization has strong values and the individual member is not open to change.[13] This seems to be the common response of pastors in America, as the average pastor's tenure is around four years. This may not be as tragic as it seems if the pastor eventually finds a ministry more congruent with his vision and values. The real tragedy is when the pastor drops out of ministry altogether.

Plant a church. When a pastor plants a church by approaching people and encouraging them to join him in his endeavor (what I refer to in church planting as a *cold start*), his core values become the core values of the church. People visit and those whose values align often stay, while those with different values either stay and try to change his values or leave.

Pursue values resolution. A fifth option is to attempt values resolution, rather than just walk out as some leaders do or abandon a ministry altogether. When values differ, a pastor or other ministry leader should at the very least attempt to resolve the differences.

Resolving Differences

The goal of values discovery is to determine an individual's and an organization's vital beliefs. When this happens, the person or ministry will develop these values into a statement or credo. However, before you move to the values-development phase, you must pass through a values-resolution phase.

The values-discovery process will often surface values conflicts. David Johnson will discover that he has harmful and helpful values and that some may contradict others. For example, he may value relevant Bible exposition. He regularly comes up with a good idea but must search, often in vain, for a biblical text to support it. Thus he does a lot of prooftexting. While this may not seem that harmful, over time it leads to preaching his ideas rather than God's truth. In addition, when he does preach the Scriptures, he may fail to show their relevance to today's world. Although he sees the need for relevance, he never quite gets to it.

Hope Community Church will also discover values conflicts. The board may discover that they hold few values in common. The older board members have a deep commitment to prayer, whereas the younger members see its importance but admit that it has not been a high priority for them and probably will not be in the future. The board may value creativity and innovation in the youth ministry: "If our youth pastor does not show a lot of creativity, we will lose our kids!" However, they are committed to maintaining the status quo in the adult ministries and worship services. This results in a mass exodus of their youth after they complete high school.

The individual or organization that ignores these conflicts pays a steep price later on. Like barnacles, values differences have a way of clinging to the organization; they refuse to go away. They will continue to raise their ugly heads until they are resolved or until the ministry disintegrates. The empty, decaying facilities of too many churches scattered all across America serve as silent reminders of people who failed to face their differences.

The values-resolution process is extremely important, and it is by no means an easy process. I would attach a label to the values-resolution package that says: Warning—this process could be dangerous to the organization's health. This is not to frighten people away from the process; it is to warn them to proceed cautiously or, as Scripture says, to be as shrewd as serpents and as innocent as doves (Matt. 10:16). Working with people's essential beliefs is like walking through a field laced with land mines. It involves dealing with emotionally charged issues that could explode and seriously scar, if not destroy, a ministry. For example, church people hold strong opinions over values issues, such as traditional versus contemporary worship styles, the exercise of the sign gifts, a woman's role in the church, lordship salvation, involvement in a small group, and so on. Working with and resolving these issues will prove to be time consuming, physically tiring, and emotionally painful.

While the values-resolution process must take place after you unearth your values, it will occur periodically throughout the life of the ministry as well. A situation will arise, often problematic, in which values will appear to conflict with one another, and the leadership will have to practice values resolution. In Acts 6:1–6, the Jerusalem church practiced values resolution when the Grecian Jews complained that the Hebraic Jews were overlooking their widows in the distribution of food (v. 1). The Twelve (the leadership) met to deal with the value, namely that their people, especially their elderly widows, are important. Their decision to turn this responsibility over to others affirmed this value but freed them to focus on what for them were more important values, prayer and the ministry of the Word (vv. 2–4).

How do you resolve these issues? What is involved in values resolution? Resolving values is much the same as resolving conflicts, as happened in Acts 6. At the heart of conflict is a difference in values. While I do not intend for this to be a major section on values resolution, here are a few suggestions.

1. Agree to pray over your differences and, specifically, pray for one another. James 5:16 says, "Therefore confess your sins to each other and pray for each other so that you may be healed. The prayer of a righteous man is powerful and effective." Bathe all that you do in prayer. Do not underestimate the power of God to heal and change lives and opinions. Do not be surprised if he changes yours.

2. Get together as a group and study the Scriptures. Begin by asking such foundational questions as, What is the purpose of the church? Why are we here? What are we supposed to be doing? What do the answers to these questions tell us about our values? According to Hebrews 4:12, God's Word has a way of getting to the hearts of men and women as well as to the heart of an issue. If the conflict is over personalities, as conflicts often are, rather than values, Scripture will reveal this.

3. Discuss your differences. Sprinkled through the book of Acts are various church conflicts (Acts 6:1–6; 15:1–21, 36–41). Most often you can resolve issues through discussion (6:2; 15:7). People must take time to listen to one another and try to see the situation from the other viewpoints. Look at those who differ with you as significant brothers and sisters in the faith, not as enemies to be slain in verbal combat.

4. Pursue consensus, not compromise. Usually compromise satisfies no one. As much as possible, agree to disagree in your attempt to arrive at the truth. The Jerusalem church did not compromise on the issue of circumcision and faith in Acts 15. They came to a consensus. They decided that a Gentile does not have to become a cultural Jew to be saved. A compromise would have changed the course of Christianity. There are times when consensus is impossible and you feel that you must go your separate ways, as with Paul and Barnabas (vv. 39–40).

5. Use an intermediary or a facilitator. The apostles, Jerusalem elders, and James served in much this capacity in Acts 15. While there is no guarantee that all parties will agree, the presence of an intermediary should help prevent any personal attacks, eliminate subjective baggage, and keep everyone focused on the issues. Some denominations provide such people as a service to their member churches.

6. Leaders must lead. This means that they will have to make some hard choices, risk offending certain people, stand up to criticism, and possibly see certain individuals and groups leave the organization. Good leadership does not immerse you in a popularity

contest. Regardless of the circumstances, leaders must do what is right. James models this kind of leadership in Acts 15:13–21; the Twelve exemplify it in Acts 6. Too many church boards see their role as the keepers of the peace. They have convinced themselves that their job is to keep everyone happy all of the time. This sends a message to astute troublemakers that they can get their way simply by complaining. They have been around churches long enough to realize that the squeaky wheel gets the grease.

Aspirational Values

Chapter 2 taught that values can be actual or aspirational. Now we must answer the question, What do we do with our aspirational values?

The Danger of Listing Aspirational Values

To include aspirational values in one's list of ministry values or credo, whether personal or congregational, has the potential of miscommunicating and being misunderstood. When you create a credo that is a list of your so-called values, people assume that you are attempting to communicate your actual values. Consequently, when you include your aspirational values, you risk congregational cynicism and alienation. People perceive that you are saying that you hold to values that you really do not own. This reeks of insincerity and comes across as empty and meaningless.

For the longest time, when I helped church leadership teams discover their values, I would not let them include any aspirational values in their final statement. I used the paragraph above to make my case. However, a number of them wanted to include in some way their aspirational values. They wanted their people to know what they aspired to as well as what they actually valued. This made sense to me, and eventually I changed my approach. I found that the solution is to discover and include aspirational values in the credo but note that they are aspirational, not actual.

The Discovery of Aspirational Values

How might you discover your personal or ministry's aspirational values? Probably the best approach is to compare your actual values with those found in a balanced, biblically functioning, spiritually healthy church. Then ask, What is missing? An example of such a church would be the Jerusalem church described in Acts 2:42–47. A reading of this passage reveals that the church held to at least six values—or possibly five if prayer is included under worship, and four if fellowship and community are combined (these are listed in appendix A). These four or five values are pretty basic to most good churches. When you compare your personal or congregational ministry values with these, where do you come up short? The answer should be your aspirational values.

Listing Aspirational Values

How might you include these values in your credo without risking inauthenticity? Select no more than two aspirational values to include with the six actual values in your credo.

Introduce the two groups of values. For example, you could introduce your actual values with: "As a church we are committed to the following values" and list them. To introduce your aspirational values you could write: "As a church we aspire to the following values" and list them. Another approach would be to mark the aspirational values in some way, such as with an asterisk and an explanation in a note. For an example, see Northwood Community Church's values credo in appendix A.

Questions for Reflection and Discussion

1. According to this chapter, who in your ministry is responsible for discovering its vital values? Who is the point person? Who are the key decision makers? Whom else should you include?
2. What are the point person's core organizational values? What are the essential values that other leaders or key decision makers hold? What are the core values of the congregation or others such as the employees? How do you know this information?
3. Do you believe that it is necessary to discover your values? Why or why not? Can you come up with reasons other than those given in this chapter?
4. If you had some trouble answering question 2, and most do, you need to conduct a values audit. You should do this now before reading the rest of this book. And you must answer several questions before you begin. Will you discover various individuals' key values first or those of the organization? Do you plan to surface the values of any under-the-umbrella organizations? Why or why not?

5. What values-discovery technique(s) will help the key decision makers to discover their individual core values? Will they need some preparation in approaching this assignment, such as a brief look at the sample credos in the appendixes of this book?
6. Are you new to the ministry or have you been previously involved in it? What values-discovery technique(s) will help you discover the organization's values and/or the under-the-umbrella organizations' beliefs? Have you collected any credos that might help you in this process?
7. Write down all the values, helpful and harmful, you have discovered. Does each pass the test of a good value? If no, why not?
8. Will you compare and communicate the results of the discovery process? Why or why not? Will you use the intersecting circles, a bar graph, or some other approach? To whom will you communicate the results? Why?
9. Did you discover any conflicting or harmful values? Identify them. Will you need to work through a values-resolution process? (Most do, although church plants may be exceptions.) Did you skip the values-resolution step? If so, why? If you went through the process, are you satisfied with the results and the process itself? If not, do it again (I know it can be painful).

4

WRITING YOUR VALUES CREDO
THE DEVELOPMENT OF CORE VALUES

Pastor David Johnson received a mailer from the seminary where he graduated that featured the brand-new continuing education class "How to Discover Your Ministry Values." Within an hour he was online, e-mailing his registration to the seminary. While the course was not expensive, he would have paid top dollar for its content. After the harsh, painful experience at Hope Community Church, he realized that to continue in ministry without a firm grasp of his essential beliefs was to invite ministry disaster.

Since completing the class, he has done some hard spadework and unearthed his personal core values. He has also decided that his future ministry will involve planting a church. He realizes that his core values will likely become the organization's values. His next goal is to shape or develop these values. This involves writing them down on paper. The finished product will be his personal values credo, which in most cases will become the church's values credo.

But how should we or David Johnson approach values development? What is involved in articulating a core values statement, or credo, for yourself or for a ministry organization such as a church? Writing a significant credo involves both preparation and a process.

The Preparation for Articulating the Values Credo

Some preparation must take place before you write a credo. This preparation is threefold. It answers the questions, Who develops the values that make up the values statement? What values are included? Why write them down?

Who Develops the Values?

Someone must assume responsibility for developing the values that make up the values statement. Essentially, the buck stops at the top. While the point person in the ministry may pass the responsibility on to someone else, ultimately he or she is directly responsible. In the church this would be the senior pastor. Should something go wrong, should there be a ministry catastrophe, the leader of the leaders must answer to the organization as a whole. I believe that the point leader should not pass this function on to another but should be directly involved in the values-shaping process. He or she should involve others but not defer to others. It is most difficult to lead an organization that operates on someone else's values.

If someone surveyed a number of known, successful organizations, such as those that make up the Fortune 500 group, he or she would quickly note that the values that mold many of those organizations have grown out of the character and leadership of one person. Examples of such leaders are Thomas Watson of IBM, Bill Gates of Microsoft Corporation, Lee Iacocca of Chrysler Corporation, Sam Walton of Wal-Mart, Walt Disney, and so on. The same holds true for many church and parachurch ministries. Bill Bright's values have influenced Campus Crusade for Christ. Billy Graham's have affected the Billy Graham Evangelistic Association. Dr. W. A. Criswell's have influenced First Baptist Church of Dallas.

Shaping robust beliefs is preeminently the responsibility of the point person. In an entrepreneurial start, whether a church, parachurch, or marketplace organization, the beliefs will be those of the corporate planter. He or she carries a mental picture or vision of what the future organization will look like, as well as the values that undergird the vision. As the dream becomes a reality, so do the essential beliefs that inform that ministry. As we saw from the research, those who join these ministries usually accept the beliefs or look for another ministry.

In an established work, a new leader will face values that often differ from his or her own. This may be disastrous, as in Pastor David's ministry at Hope Community Church. The leader of leaders will attempt to mold some new values. In the church he must draft and involve others (a ministry team) in the process. This is the new ministry paradigm mentioned in chapter 3. The amount of that involvement depends to some degree on the nature and size of the ministry. Churches are nonprofit, volunteer organizations. Thus much of their ministry is dependent on volunteer lay leadership at various levels in the church, especially in small churches. In these churches, at least the pastor, the board, and those who lead ministries should be a part of the process of molding new values.

I suggest a bottom-to-top approach. People who are lower down in the organization often have much insight into the real values that have catalyzed past ministry success. Also, when leaders at various lower ministry levels exercise their creativity, innovation, and initiative, they feel they make a difference and their ministry becomes more meaningful. This also allows them to get their fingerprints all over the process, and they feel greater ownership. But what if they come up with some off-the-wall values, or they suggest different or contradictory values? This could happen if they work from a clean slate. If you think this might be a problem, then draft the initial set of values congruent with the ministry vision and put them in a values statement. Then encourage the other leaders to examine the values set. That involves granting them permission to add to, change, or leave the statement intact. Most often the statement will not change appreciably, and the changes that you adopt will be good ones based on common cause.

Not only does the ministry develop values that direct it as a whole, but any ministries that are a part of the broader ministry should follow suit. Here is where others play a strong role in values formation. With the overall credo in place as a guide, they will carve a unique set of beliefs for their particular ministry. The point person, who works directly in these services, knows them best and should influence the beliefs.

What Values?

What values will you shape? The leadership and individuals involved in the values-development process need to mold their own personal and organizational beliefs while they are in the process of doing the same for the ministry institution. They must work with their actual values, not aspirational ones; and they must be congruent, not contradictory. In short, they are the biblical beliefs that have cleared through the values-discovery and resolution processes. They are the values that, like pieces of raw clay, the leadership will mold and shape into a sculpted form that should communicate with and catalyze those in the ministry, as well as the leaders themselves.

In some cases, the values derive from founding roots. These describe new or entrepreneurial church ministries. Most likely, they are not new values but are new to the ministry. The struggle is deciding whether they are actual or aspirational values. Perhaps at this point in the new ministry's life it is appropriate to have aspirational beliefs. Only the test of time and ministry development will prove what is actual and what is aspirational.

In some cases, the beliefs come from second-generation organizations or were dormant and have been recently rekindled. This describes the values of established churches that leadership, usually new leadership, has in some way revitalized. A new leader has come on the scene and found that the church was built on some very significant beliefs, but the past leadership has allowed those beliefs to burn down to a mere spark. Gradually over the years, the life has oozed out of them. These values have easily worked their way through the discovery and resolution process because the congregation already owns them. The values-development process will either dust them off or provide them with a needed face-lift, and the values-communication stage will recast them.

In other cases, the values have grown old and become tired. Fresh values may replace some, or they may need a face-lift; that is, they need to be reworded in relevant, contemporary language that communicates them in fresh ways in the twenty-first century. But how can you know if your ministry is suffering from tired values? How can you know if you need to change your values or give them a face-lift?

There are no fewer than seven warning signals that reveal the unhealthy state of the church's vital signs. One is frequent confusion and disagreement among the organization's leaders or top decision makers, as well as among the organization's constituency, over various issues, such as programs, techniques, styles of ministry, and so on. Things are no longer the way they used to be in the good old days, and much disagreement exists over how to cope with this phenomenon.

Another warning signal is overt cynicism and pessimism of many toward the organization's future. They are not sure that it has a future. A third warning signal is a corporate reputation for maintenance ministry. The people are in a survival mode. The church is exhausted, and all its efforts are aimed at keeping the doors open.

A plateaued or declining attendance is another warning. In a church people may be coming not because they want to but because they feel they have to. As one looks out across the congregation, one notes that most are wonderful elderly people. Few young people are present, and many of them will leave when they graduate from high school or go off to college.

There are three more warning signals. People in the ministry are going through the motions. The preaching lacks power and vibrancy. Not much commitment exists among the people. They are doing their duty—showing up and dropping some money in the offering plate—but nothing more. A strong resistance to change and innovation is a warning signal. No one is willing to take any risks. The organization does not see the need for change or simply refuses to change, preferring to see the organization die than to risk the pain of change. Finally, poor communication from the leadership to those in the organization, which in turn invites a lack of trust, is a warning signal. The board does not trust the founder, the deacon board has lost confidence in the pastor, the people do not trust the board, and no one is talking to the other parties involved.

Organizational values need a face-lift when there is:

- Frequent confusion and disagreement
- Overt cynicism and pessimism
- A maintenance ministry
- Plateaued or declining attendance
- A lack of commitment and enthusiasm
- Low tolerance of change
- Distrust of leadership

Why Write the Values Down?

There are several benefits to written values statements. One is that a written credo infuses the values with leadership authority. Dave Francis and Mike Woodcock write, "Values will not have the authority to be a leadership statement until they are clear enough to be committed to paper."[1] When the beliefs of the organization are penned in ink and communicated to all its people, no one can plead ignorance in a values violation. The leadership has the authority to expect compliance from all who make up the ministry organization. Those who choose to ignore or violate the ministry beliefs do so in direct disobedience of the leadership and subject themselves to discipline or termination.

Francis and Woodcock's statement suggests another advantage—clarity. Written communication is much clearer and more precise than spoken communication. The ear does not hear nor does the mind remember as well as what the eye sees in front of it. Writing down the core beliefs forces the congregation to clarify precisely what it believes. Then if any problems exist, it is not because of any question over what someone said but over one's interpretation of what is clearly and precisely written.

Writing down the values in the development stage communicates precisely what came out of the discovery and resolution process. It allows people to discover if their understanding is the same as the team's interpretation. If any questions or interpretive disagreements exist, they will surface when the values are written out. At that point, the developers can discuss and if need be debate them further to arrive at common ground.

Writing down core beliefs is vital to communicating those beliefs. It is the first step of the communication process. Even in what has become a multisensory culture, writing remains fundamental to good communication. While the leadership will attempt to communicate the ministry's values in numerous ways, it cannot ignore written communication.

The Process of Articulating the Credo

Several steps make up the process of writing a values credo for an individual or a congregation.

Determine the Value, Not Its Form

The first step involves determining the value itself, not the form it will take. As I discussed in chapter 2, the form is the means by which the value is realized. To return to a familiar illustration, some ministries such as churches list small groups as a value. Actually, the small group meeting is not the value but the form that the value may take. The real value behind many contemporary small-group programs of the 1990s is authentic biblical community.

Value	Form
Biblical community	Small groups
Evangelism	Knocking on doors
Fellowship	Home Bible study

To mistakenly articulate a form of the value rather than the value itself will affect the constancy of the values statement. Values are constant, change-resistant things. They should not change appreciably over the life of a ministry. The forms the values take, however, are not constant, nor should they be. Scripture determines core values but does not dictate the forms those values take. There are no biblical forms that Christians must follow. Some argue that not only must believers do what the Bible says, but they must do it the way the church did it in the first century. If this were true, it would lock the church into a first-century culture. This is the mistake that the Amish have made, except they have locked themselves into the culture of the eighteenth or nineteenth century, not that of the first century. Either way, the church becomes culturally irrelevant; it fails to address the issues of its culture and has very little impact.

If, in writing the credo, the form of the value is included and not the value, the credo will change every time the ministry makes an adjustment to its culture. The organization may want to include the form as well as the value in the credo, but it should make the distinction clear. Here is an example:

> *A Commitment to Authentic Biblical Community*
> We believe that we are responsible as the body of Christ to provide contexts where all of our people can experience authentic biblical community. For us authentic community is relationship building, spiritual growth stimulation, and leadership development. We desire to accomplish this through an active, robust network of small groups that will meet all over the city and accommodate people of all ages in our church.

Later, should the ministry desire to accomplish community in another way, they can replace the last sentence with the new method.

Determine the Number of Values

The next step is to determine the number of values that will go into the personal or organizational credo and their priority. The important, controlling question is, How many beliefs should make up the statement of values? A quick survey of the values statements found in the appendixes and other sources is instructive. The least number of values is one. Hewlett-Packard, a marketplace organization, states: "The HP Way says, 'Do unto others as you would have them do to you.' That's really what it's all about."[2]

The next lowest number is three. There are two examples that are both from marketplace organizations. The first is the business of Ken Blanchard, a Christian and president and CEO of Blanchard Training and Development in Escondido, California. According to *Compass,* a publication of the Leadership Network, Blanchard leads his company according to three core values: "Ethical (doing the right things), relationships (building mutually satisfying partnerships with our people), and success (accomplishing our established company goals)."[3] The second is from Thomas J. Watson Jr., who was the chairman of the board of International Business Machines Corporation (IBM). In his book *A Business and Its Beliefs,* he identifies his three deep beliefs for IBM: "respect for the individual, major attention to service, drive for superiority in all things."[4]

The organization in the appendixes with the most values is Saddleback Valley Community Church in Orange County, California. Their philosophy of ministry, found in appendix A, lists seventeen values. CAM International, in appendix B, has fifteen.

The rest of the values in the appendixes cluster within a range of three to ten. The majority (five credos) have six values. The next highest number (four credos) have seven, and two credos have nine. The church credos have the most core values. They range from three to seventeen. Most churches, however, have between six and nine values. The marketplace credos have the fewest essential values. The range was from one to twelve, with most between three and six.

In *Built to Last,* James Collins and Jerry Porras address the ideal number of values that an organization should have from a marketplace perspective. They explain, "If you articulate more than five or six, there's a good chance you're not getting down to only the core essentials."[5] They write, "Visionary companies tend to have only a few core values, usually between three and six. In fact, we found none of the visionary companies to have more than six core values, and most have less."[6] Their findings agree with mine, contrary to Francis and Woodcock, who argue for at least twelve. This is why I limit the churches that I consult with to six actual and two aspirational values, and that may be stretching things. Less is better, and in the case of ministry values, less is core.

The work of Collins and Porras and the church credos in appendix A suggest that the ideal church credo contains six to nine core values. An acceptable range is five to ten. Fewer than five would seem to ignore some crucial biblical values as found in the Jerusalem church's credo in appendix A. More than ten, however, would seem to get away from the organization's core essentials, dissipate people's energy, and ultimately confuse them. If you have more than ten values in your personal or organizational credo, review them several times, asking the question, What is core to this organization? Another question is, Should any values be combined under a common value? If you have fewer than five, review some of the church credos in appendix A to see if you missed some vital values.

Having said all this, however, the final verdict on the number of values lies with the people in the organization. If they find common cause and are excited about two or three values or as many as fifteen values, they should go with that number. You must remember that the final judge of the number of values in the credo is the people who must minister in the organization—from the occasional volunteer worker to the primary ministry leader. CAM International is an example. Around 250 missionaries took part in determining the mission's core beliefs. They all agreed on fifteen precepts, no more, no less (appendix B).

Saddleback Valley Community Church, with seventeen core beliefs, proves to be the exception for all three groups: churches, parachurches, and marketplace organizations. A quick review of their credo in appendix A demonstrates what for them are vital values. In the values-discovery process, you should discover as many of your values as possible so that you may be aware of all that is driving your organization. The next step is to study those values and ask, What is core? As I review Saddleback's credo, all seem important. I suspect that much like CAM International, the staff and people at Saddleback have determined these values and feel that they are central to their excellent ministry.

When you have determined the number of values, arrange them in order of priority, for two reasons. First, this reflects their importance to the ministry. The most important ones appear early in the list. I suspect that when a person initially lists personal values or those of an organization, he or she naturally lists the most important at the beginning. Those are the ones that come to mind first. It is not clear if any of the credos in the appendixes are in order of priority. Several ministries place a commitment to Scripture as the first priority. This makes sense because all the other values are based on Scripture as the Word of God.

The second reason for listing the values in order of priority is that all truth is not of equal importance for every purpose, and it is unlikely that people can behave in a consistent way with each of their values all the time. Therefore, the earlier values communicate what is important and where people will focus their energies and strive most for common cause.

Determine the Format of the Values

A quick glance at the credos in the appendixes reveals that core beliefs can be stated in a number of different ways. However, the general rule is to keep them "simple, clear, straightforward, and powerful."[7] Your goal is to define clearly your beliefs in a significant way that people understand. The leader is most important here. He or she should have a feel for what is most effective within the organization—what best grabs people's attention and is meaningful, compelling, and appealing rationally and emotionally.

I recommend that the written value have three components: an introduction, an explanation, and a scriptural validation.

INTRODUCE THE VALUE

First, there should be a lead statement or heading that identifies or introduces the value. Appendix A provides several samples. Grace Community Bible Church of Richmond, Texas, uses the same four words to introduce their values: "A Dedication to (value)." Lakeview Community Church of Cedar Hill, Texas, identifies each value with "A Commitment to (value)." Saddleback Valley Community Church introduces each core value with "We Value (value)." To this, Grand Blanc Community Church of Grand Blanc, Michigan, adds an adverb, "We deeply value (value)." Willow Creek Community Church of South Barrington, Illinois, heads each value with "We believe that (value)."

Others word these differently. Fellowship Bible Church of Dallas uses such headings as: A Philosophy of Grace, A Christian Self-Image, Biblical Authority, Communicating Christ to the Contemporary Culture, and so on. Carroll Community Church in Westminster, Maryland, begins each heading with a verb: Love Jesus Christ, Be Connected through a Small Group, Build Friendships with Non-Christians, and so on.

EXPLAIN THE VALUE

The second component is a concise explanation of the value. Grace Community Bible Church accomplishes this with one sentence.

A Dedication to Purpose

Our purpose is to lead people to salvation in Christ and growth in Christ-likeness.

A Dedication to People

God works through people, and each person is unique and vital to God's plan.

Fellowship Bible Church varies from one to several sentences.

A Philosophy of Grace

You cannot earn God's acceptance. He accepts you now and forever through faith in Jesus Christ. The church should not focus on guilt to motivate its members, but encourage them to live good lives from a motivation of love and thankfulness toward the Lord.

A Christian Self-Image

You can have a positive self-image, not because of who you are in yourself, but because of what God has done for you in Jesus Christ.

Carroll Community Church is similar to Fellowship Bible Church.

Love Jesus Christ

No one can love God for us. We must individually stay connected to Christ through an abiding relationship (John 15). Through the Word of God, prayer, personal worship, and obedience we can love God with heart, soul, mind, and strength.

Be Connected through a Small Group

Community groups help us develop caring relationships with one another. In this small-group context we can get to know people, hold each other accountable, and offer newcomers a place to belong.

Willow Creek Community Church presents each value in one sentence.

We believe that anointed teaching is the catalyst for transformation in individuals' lives and in the church.

We believe that lost people matter to God, and, therefore, ought to matter to the church.

We believe that the church should be culturally relevant while remaining doctrinally pure.

Lakeview Community Church presents the value and follows it with a "so what" statement signaled by the word *therefore*. The "so what" communicates what difference the value will make in the life of the church or how the core belief applies to the church's ministries.

A Commitment to Prayer

We believe that God desires his people to pray and that he hears and answers prayer (Matt. 7:7–11; James 5:13–18). *Therefore,* the ministries and activities of this church will be characterized by a reliance on prayer in their conception, planning, and execution [italics mine].

A Commitment to Lay Ministry

We believe that the primary responsibility of the pastor(s) and teachers in the local church is to "prepare God's people for works of service" (Eph. 4:12). *Therefore,* the ministry of Lakeview Community Church will be placed as much as possible in the hands of nonvocational workers. This will be accomplished through training opportunities and through practices which encourage lay initiation, leadership, responsibility, and authority in the various ministries of the church [italics mine].

VALIDATE THE VALUE

The third component is one or two passages of Scripture that validate the value. This communicates that the value is biblical and that what this organization believes is based on the Bible. However, you must be leery of prooftexting. Make sure that you have legitimate biblical substantiation for all your beliefs. A brief survey of appendix A reveals that most credos have no Scripture references (the references are assumed), some have a few, and two have references for all of their values.

Lakeview Community Church includes Scripture in some values. The two sample beliefs above for prayer and lay ministry illustrate this recommendation.

Parkview Evangelical Free Church cites a biblical reference for all three beliefs. Here are two:

Scripture

A biblical message: We are committed to the clear and accurate communication of God's Word in a way that ministers grace and urges obedience (2 Tim. 3:16–17).

Creativity

A fresh approach: We are committed to forms of worship and ministry that will best capture and express what God is doing in our generation and culture (Luke 5:33–39).

Saddleback Valley Community Church also includes a scriptural reference for each value. It cites anywhere from one to as many as five passages for a core belief.

We Value the Application of Scripture

"Do not merely listen to the word, and so deceive yourselves. Do what it says" (James 1:22).

We Value Feedback

"A fool thinks he needs no advice, but a wise man listens to others" (Prov. 12:15 TLB).

"Get the facts at any price" (Prov. 23:23 TLB).

"Every prudent man acts out of knowledge" (Prov 13:16).

"Be sure you know the condition of your flocks, give careful attention to your herds" (Prov. 27:23).

"Reliable communication permits progress" (Prov. 13:17 TLB).

The way you write your credo does not need to be unique. I suggest that you work your way through the credos in the appendixes, looking for a format that best suits your tastes and that of your organization. You may find one credo style that meets all your needs, or you may want to draw from several.

Whatever you decide, two principles may prove helpful. Both concern the idea that like attracts like. One is that you are intuitively attracted to core values formats that fit your tastes. For example, as you browse through the credos, some will virtually jump off the page and grab your attention. Others merely sit there and vegetate.

The other principle is that you are intuitively attracted to credos from ministries that are what you envision for your ministry. If you are involved in an entrepreneurial work, it is where you are taking your ministry; if you are in an established work, it is where you would like to take your ministry. Many people identify with a ministry that for them represents the ideal. It also has leaders who for them are ideal leaders and serve as heroes. This is healthy and good. And it is their credos that attract them.

The Test of a Well-Written Credo

How can you know whether your credo is well written? A well-worded values statement should attract interest, instill pride, communicate well, and include a limited number of values. Actually, the development process never ends entirely. You should periodically review the statement with these characteristics in mind, constantly seeking to improve it.

ATTRACTS INTEREST

Does your credo attract people's interest? You should articulate the values in the credo in such a way that they attract people's positive attention. The way you accomplish this is to pay attention to the language you use. The values statements must be well worded. Use fresh, descriptive words that uplift and inspire the spirit. Avoid tired and worn-out language. Articulating what your organization stands for should not result in the verbal equivalent of chicken broth as the main meal—bland and unappealing.

One reason a credo in the appendixes may attract your attention is its language. For example Lakeview Community Church's first value says, "The Bible is both timeless and timely, relevant to the common needs of all people at all times and to the specific problems of contemporary living." Willow Creek Community Church's second value states, "We believe that lost people matter to God, and, therefore, ought to matter to the church." Francis and Woodcock attract attention with such statements as: Managers must manage. Cream belongs at the top. Do the right thing. Do things right. Who cares wins. Who dares wins. Know thine enemy. There are no free lunches.

Another way a credo can attract interest is its brevity. Remember: Less is more. Keep it short and to the point, because today's multi-image, multisensory culture reads less. If people see relatively few words on a page, they tend to read the page, but they will avoid a page that's full of text. (For example, think about how you read through the newspaper. Do you often skip over the longer articles and advertisements?) The advertising world refers to the space around text as *white space*. People tend to read material when there is a lot of white space, not lots of text.

INSTILLS PRIDE

Does your credo instill pride in the people who make up the organization? The term *pride* usually has a negative connotation in Christian circles. Here I use it in a positive sense. Values should instill pride by making people in the organization feel good to be a part of the organization as opposed to feeling embarrassed. The words must encourage and uplift people. Those who make up the ministry should believe that they are part of an organization that is going to make a significant difference in their community or world for the Savior. See the first two values of Fellowship Bible Church. They instill pride.

COMMUNICATES WELL

Does your credo communicate clearly to your organization and its ministry audience? Leaders are responsible for translating values into terms that people can understand. As above, the words people use and the ways they use them have impact. Leaders must understand their community and its culture if what they communicate is to speak with relevance. Using clear, precise language is imperative. The terms that you would use with an uneducated community will probably be different from those you'd use with a highly educated community. Communicate in the language of your people and your target audience.

I suggest that several people read your credo to determine if it communicates well. Ask people in the organization as well as people outside the ministry what they think it says. Also, you may want someone from your target community to read it. The key questions are, Do they all understand? If they don't, why not?

HAS A LIMITED NUMBER OF VALUES

Do you have too many values in your credo? A good values statement should convey to all what an individual or ministry believes is important. As I said earlier, the general rule, on the one hand, is to have enough values so that the credo does not appear vague and unfocused. On the other hand, having too many values often results in a loss of clarity and dissipation of people's energy.

The Test of a Well-Written Credo

- Does it attract interest?
- Does it instill pride?
- Does it communicate well?
- Does it include a limited number of values?

Questions for Reflection and Discussion

1. Who has the responsibility for developing the values in your church, ministry, or work? Is it the point person (senior pastor, president, CEO)? Why or why not? Does this person really want to shape the values? How much input comes from those on a lower leadership level?

2. Have you discovered your personal values for your ministry? If not, why not? Have you begun to write them down in the form of a credo? Why or why not? Have you discovered the values of the church you are interested or involved in? Have you begun to develop them?

3. Are you part of a new or an established ministry? If you are part of a new ministry, such as a church plant or a new ministry within the church, what must you be aware of in terms of your beliefs? If you are involved in an established ministry, do you have any tired values? Are any of the warning signs that serve as a ministry's vital signs true of this ministry?

4. Are you convinced that you need to articulate a values credo? Why is it important that you write a values statement? Have you begun the process? If you have not, do you plan to do so soon? When? What are you waiting for?

5. What is the difference between a value's function and its form? What are two ways that help you to capture the essence of a value and not its form? Is it ever okay to include the value's form in the values statement?

6. If you are part of a church or even a parachurch organization, what is the least number of values that should appear in your credo? What is the most? Do you believe that your ministry's credo has too many or too few beliefs? Why or why not?

7. Have you selected a particular format for your credo? If you have not, why not? Does it meet the three criteria suggested in this chapter? Are you able to create a fresh, new credo, or do you need to use the credos in the appendixes to stimulate your creativity? Do you have a ministry organization that serves as an ideal for you? If so, do they have a written credo and would it help in writing yours?

8. If you have written a credo or when you finish writing one, it should pass the test of a well-written credo. What are the three parts of this test? Does your statement pass each part? If not, why not?

5

MOVING YOUR VALUES FROM PAPER TO PEOPLE
THE COMMUNICATION OF CORE VALUES

A pastor could develop the perfect values statement for a congregation. It could meet or even exceed all the requirements in the last chapter. That leader could read through the credo and be struck, even emotionally overwhelmed, by its excellence. He might even stand back, shake his head, and say, "Wow, this is outstanding!" However, if the ministry's constituency does not know what those values are, if the leader has not taken the time to clearly communicate them, it would be difficult, if not impossible, for the organization to implement them.

Pastor David Johnson is in the process of planting an exciting new paradigm church in a growing suburb about fifteen miles north of Dallas and about twenty-five miles northwest of the community of Little Hope. He is surprised at and feels a little overwhelmed by the large number of people who have responded to his mailers and ads in the area newspaper and who have expressed a strong interest in being a part of the core group. He has begun a series of informal meetings to impart to these prospects and other interested parties the new church's DNA (core values, mission, vision, and strategy).

Meanwhile, Hope Community Church has not been sitting idly by waiting to die the slow, painful death I previously predicted. The divorce hurt them as well, and they also learned some painful lessons about the importance of core values. Currently they are seeking a pastor. The board enlisted the aid of the same faculty person who taught David how to discover his key beliefs. After some hard work, they now have a well-written credo as well as a significant vision that has proved vital in their pastoral search and has led them to an older, semiretired man.

Now the problem for Pastor David and for the leadership at Hope Community Church is to move the credos from paper to people. He and they must ask, How do we get the values off the paper on which they are written and into the minds and hearts of those who make up the ministry organization? They realize that what they have articulated on paper, though extremely important to the vitality and future of the ministry, will prove impotent if it does not penetrate their people. But what is the simplest, most powerful, most memorable way to communicate their precepts? The purpose of this chapter is to explain the values-casting process and provide some practical methods for communicating the bottom-line beliefs to the ministry community and the ministry constituency.

The Values-Casting Process

Communicating the contents of a potent, compelling credo is similar to conveying a profound, significant vision for the future of an organization. Both processes involve a sender, a message, and a receiver. These are communication basics and vital to the values- and vision-casting processes. The ministry congregation should think through these three areas if they are to effectively convey their cherished beliefs.

The Senders

The first step in the values-casting process is to decide who is formally and informally responsible for conveying the shaping values. This is not a problem for most gifted leaders. However, some who have the responsibility for getting the job done struggle with that responsibility. As in the previous chapters, the primary responsibility is with everyone who is a part of the organization (the E. F. Hutton people): the point person and any staff, the board, and the other key decision makers who comprise the ministry team.

THE POINT PERSON

The primary responsibility for sending the core values, mission, and vision of a ministry organization lies with its point person. This is natural because in most circumstances he or she is the primary representative and spokesperson for the organization. In the church this person will be the senior pastor in larger churches and the only pastor in smaller churches. In the parachurch the spokesperson is often the president or even a chancellor.

One of the primary functions of an organizational leader is the casting of the core values and vision. This function is an expectation in most parachurch and marketplace organizations. For example, the president of a theological seminary or a missions agency is responsible for traveling and representing that agency—its values and vision—to its constituents and interested parties. This has not been true, however, of the majority of churches in the twentieth and now in the twenty-first century. The typical small church, which makes up the majority of churches sprinkled all across North American soil, views the pastor as the hired hand. While Ephesians 4:11–13 teaches that all in the church, laypeople as well as professionals, are gifted and responsible for ministry, the pastor is the one that "we hired to do the ministry."[1] Many see the pastor's position as an office, and his job description consists of such responsibilities as preaching and teaching; counseling; administration; home and hospital visitation; and conducting the ordinances, funerals, and weddings. Some would include leadership; others would leave that with the board and view him as the board's employee.

None of the above is found in the Scriptures. No office of pastor exists, only the gift (Rom. 12:7; 1 Cor. 12:28–29; Eph. 4:11). The Bible does not assign these responsibilities to one person but to those in the body of Christ. Where did this hired-hand concept come from? It is primarily cultural. In fact, 85 to 90 percent of what the typical church does today is influenced by its culture (the church's culture, not necessarily that of the community), not the Bible. However, that does not mean that having a pastor and asking him to preach and teach and assume some of these other responsibilities is wrong or contrary to Scripture. The Bible gives the church more freedom and flexibility in this area than most realize.

I am suggesting that the church of Jesus Christ be open to new paradigms and ways of doing ministry in the twenty-first century. The Scriptures allow for, perhaps even encourage, this. The church needs the professional pastor at the head of its ministry, not at the feet of its board. But I argue that he, as well as others in the church, should be a visionary leader with the abilities to cast the vision and primary values of the ministry. This casting responsibility is threefold. First, he needs to be the vision and values cultivator. This involves initiating and developing the vision and beliefs. Second, he communicates the vision and values. This involves regularly holding them up before the congregation. Finally, he is the dream and values clarifier. This involves regularly rethinking and further refining the vision and values of the church.

THE MINISTRY TEAM

The primary leader, however, must not take sole responsibility for casting the core values and the vision. He or she must not attempt to communicate them alone. A part of the leader's responsibility is to ignite others to become values casters.

Who are these other people? Formally, they are the leaders, the key decision makers who serve at the various levels of leadership throughout the organization. In the church they are the men and women who serve on the staff, on the church board, on other boards, as teachers, as small group leaders, and so on. You must not overlook them in the casting process, for they are the very ones who are in positions to influence people at the grassroots level. Informally, they include people in the church who exert a powerful influence but not in an official capacity. They do not sit on any boards, teach any classes, nor do they lead any small groups. An example is the widow of the founding pastor, a former board member, the former pastor, the most wealthy man or woman in the church, a squeaky wheel, a retired pastor, the church patriarch or matriarch, the pastor's parents, and others. The role they play and the influence they exert may be positive or negative, and they must not be ignored in the values-casting process.

When any of these key people are involved in the process, they get their fingerprints all over it and thus gain ownership of it. My experience has been that they sense it is theirs, not just the pastor's, and this excites them. Thus they go away from the process excited about their values, and they share this with others—especially their circles of influence throughout the church. Pastors and other leaders should call this to the ownership team's attention and do everything in their power to encourage it.

SIGNIFICANT OTHERS

The significant others of an organization are the people who make up the rest of the organization. They are mostly the followers at the grassroots level—they are the grassroots. Formally, they consist of the men and women who are volunteers, official members, and regular attenders of a congregation.

A strong organization such as a church also needs an informal communications network to spread its culture, the most important part of which is its values. Informally, this network consists of what someone calls storytellers, priests, and whisperers.[2] The function of storytellers is to communicate and keep the organizational or congregational culture (particularly the values) alive by spreading stories about the organization's heroes. These heroes are the people, usually leaders, who have modeled the values during times of struggle as well as times of prosperity. The priests are the protectors of the primary values. These men and women have ownership of the values and see their importance to the life and future of the ministry. They worry about and are on the alert for the intrusion of foreign values. The whisperers transmit and thus communicate the values into inaccessible places.[3] In the church they are the ones, for example, who visit the nursing homes or have maintained contact with ministry dropouts or have networks among the unchurched community, including gays, prostitutes, drug abusers, and so on.

The wise ministry leader will accomplish more for Christ's kingdom by recruiting all the above people as values and vision casters. Together they form a coalition of communicators who can formally and informally rally the entire ministry behind the efforts of the leadership. They represent what can be an unstoppable force that practically guarantees progress toward and fulfillment of the dreams and core values of the organization.

The Message

The next part of the communication process concerns the message. The organization and the leadership must have a clear message. Three factors affect a clear message: its content, its comprehension, and its credibility.

THE CONTENTS OF THE MESSAGE

The contents of the message are the organization's DNA—its core values, mission, vision, and strategy. Some ministries, especially churches, may not have a dream, much less a vision statement, or a carefully thought-through strategy. However, all will have primary values, good or bad, but may not have articulated them in a values set or credo.

As I have already said, it is vital that every ministry have a mission and a vision statement. They provide a ministry with its direction, answering the important questions, Where is this ministry going? and What will it look like when it gets there? All organizations are mission and vision focused. They serve to bring the future into focus for both the leader and those who are a part of the corporation. Christ established the mission and vision for the church in the first century A.D. in the Great Commission. (The vision for parachurch ministries is either the Great Commission or is subsumed under it. I discuss vision casting in detail in the second edition of my book *Developing a Vision for Ministry in the 21st Century*.[4])

The focus of this book, however, is the communication of the organization's core beliefs. A leader must cast both the vision and the values. Ministries are vision focused and values driven. The dream brings the organization's direction into focus, while the values quietly, often subconsciously, move the ministry in that direction. Many of the techniques for communicating the values and vision are the same. So casting one enhances casting of the other.

THE COMPREHENSION OF THE MESSAGE

A major factor in the effective communication of any message is whether or not the audience or congregation understands it. In this case, the question is, Does your audience understand your vision and in particular your core values? Do they get it? Do they know where you are going and what is moving you in that direction? If no one understands the values, if no one gets it, as far as the organization is concerned, there might as well be no values. That does not mean that we actually have no values; they will be around regardless of people's recognition of them. However, poor casting or no casting confuses followers. It dissipates their energy, and they aren't sure where they are going.

An important factor in values casting is not only how you communicate the beliefs, but what people hear when you communicate them. We may spend much time in the careful articulation of a beliefs credo, and that is very important; however, if the audience does not hear what we intend to communicate, we are not communicating. This is Paul's point in 1 Corinthians 14:8 when he writes, "If the trumpet does not sound a clear call, who will get ready for battle?" If no one had accepted Christ as Messiah after Peter's sermon in Acts 2:14–41, he would have had to ask, What did all those people hear me say? We need to spend time not only in developing the essential values but in testing and determining what listeners are hearing.

That means that a time comes when we stop talking and start listening; or better, as we talk, we also listen. We must interlace our communicating with the audience with listening to that audience. Good communication involves good listening. One way of determining what people are receiving is to regularly ask questions of people in the organization. What does this ministry stand for? What is the congregation's bottom line? Of all that we value as a ministry, what are our essential beliefs? Then sit back and listen. Most likely, the organization's people will give you a lesson in communications, and you will make numerous adjustments in the methods you use—all to your advantage.

THE CREDIBILITY OF THE MESSAGE

A third factor that affects the clear communication of the essential beliefs is credibility. The first factor asks, What are we communicating? The second asks, Do they understand it? The third concerns, Do they believe it? A short circuit may occur anywhere in the process of casting the values. It may happen at the beginning, with the result that the values are poorly communicated. It may happen in the middle, and people simply do not get it. But it may happen as well at the end, and they simply do not believe it. Three elements lend credibility to the values-casting process: competence of the leadership, content of the message, and character of the leadership.

The first is the pastor-leader's or sender's track record. I call this competence or *performance credibility*. Receivers ask, What about the sender's past performance? Did he or she get the job done? Did he do it well? Elements that contribute to enhanced credibility are God's evident blessing on a person's life and leadership; ministry success; unique gifts, talents, and abilities; personal commitment to and passion for the cause; a strong commitment to the Scriptures; a godly life; an excellent reputation; good pulpit skills; strong people skills; ministry endurance; and others. While somewhat a mystery, God chooses to favor the ministry of some leaders. God showed special favor to Nehemiah's leadership—even the pagan king Artaxerxes was disposed to aid his ministry, as Nehemiah explains in Nehemiah 2:18 (NASB): "I told them how the hand of my God had been favorable to me, and also about the king's words which he had spoken to me."

The life and ministry of Dr. Charles Swindoll well illustrated this principle in the twentieth and now in the twenty-first century. After a long, distinguished career as a pastor, writer, and speaker on the radio program *Insight for Living,* Chuck became the fourth president of Dallas Theological Seminary. At a time when many seminaries across North America were struggling, God used him and his track record to breathe life into the seminary. Almost immediately the student population began to increase in numbers, and those who had not heard of the seminary became aware of its existence.

The second element is the content of the message. I call this *content credibility*. In this case it is the actual values that the sender communicates. The question is, When people hear the values message, does it sound credible? Several factors will influence their answer. Is the credo based on Scripture? For Christians this is a must. It is essential that core values be biblical or sacred as opposed to secular in origin. The difference is like night and day. One is based on truth and the other on falsehood. However, many values statements are based on the truth of God's Word, yet they do not all share the same credibility. Some people value one set of biblical values over another. What is the difference? The answer is a second factor—common cause. Listeners will ask, Are the organization's values my values? When people share the same key beliefs, the result is instant credibility. If I hear you espouse biblical, core values that I hold dear, you have won much credibility with me. You may hold other values that are biblical and good, yet if they are not my values, I grant you less credibility.

The third element that affects message credibility is the leader's or values caster's integrity. I refer to this as *character credibility*. Leaders and values casters who model good character and trustworthiness can expect high credibility. Those who do not will lose credibility and should not be in positions of leadership. Jesus warns believers to watch out for false prophets, and he explains that the distinguishing factor is good or bad fruit. Jesus says: "Every good tree bears good fruit, but a bad tree bears bad fruit. A good tree cannot bear bad fruit, and a bad tree cannot bear good fruit. Every tree that does not bear good fruit is cut down and thrown into the fire. Thus, by their fruit you will recognize them" (Matt. 7:17–20). Scripture instructs the church to grant credibility on the basis of strong character. First Timothy 3:1–13 and Titus 1:6–9 list character qualities for church leaders.

Character and integrity are the foundation of any Christian's leadership in general and of his or her message in particular. If the character is flawed, most believe the message to be flawed. This was demonstrated in the 1980s by the fall of a number of high-profile tel-evangelists, along with many local church pastors and a few parachurch leaders. The late 1980s and 1990s turned out to be a difficult time for those in ministry and for their organizations. Wolves in sheep's cloth-ing ravaged the cause of Christ and the credibility of the institutional church. And their personal desires and ambitions fed the Baby Bust-ers' undaunted skepticism. However, light shines most brilliantly in the midst of darkness. It is most noticeable when everything around it is dark. Those with sterling, Christ-like character stood in stark contrast to all the rest, and their credible messages had great impact for the Savior.

The Receivers

The final element of the communication process involves the re-ceiver. Receivers consist of the ministry's audience, which I divide into two groups: the ministry community and the ministry constituency. The ministry community is made up of all those who are immediately responsible for realizing the organization's primary beliefs and dream. In a parachurch ministry they are people ranging from the president to the part-time volunteer who serves only a few hours a week answering phones. In the church it is the pastor, any staff (full- and part-time), various boards, lay leaders, Sunday school teachers, members, and interested attenders.

The goal is that all of these people understand the core values and, as much as possible, share these values. Common cause is critical to the success of the ministry and the realization of its mission. The ministry community must know which values of an organization are primary or high priority. Communicating these values tells them which are core. What happens if they discover little commonality in the basic values? Since they are so central to what the corporation is all about, I suggest that the individuals leave and find a ministry where they are a better fit. To stay and attempt to cause change is a long and painful process. Unless one feels led of God to do this and is willing to go about it with a patient, loving spirit, that person would best use his or her time serving in another ministry.

The ministry constituency is made up of all those people who have some interest in the ministry but are not a part of its immediate com-munity. They are on the organization's fringe. They are people who pe-riodically pray for and contribute to the ministry. They may be relatives of those involved in some way in the ministry. Often they are people interested in becoming a part of the congregation sometime in the future. In church planting, for example, some in the ministry constituency are waiting to see if the new church will make it through the first year, or they are waiting for it to grow big enough to support a youth work for their teenagers before they join.

Good values casting means communicating to those in the ministry constituency as well as in the community. Since the ministry constitu-ency represents those who might become part of the ministry com-munity, they need to be aware of and understand the core beliefs. This knowledge could help them decide whether to get off the fence or move to other pastures.

Practical Methods for Casting the Core Values

Communication involves the task of translating primary beliefs into meaningful terms for those who are the ministry's receivers—the ministry community and constituency. While this is the responsibility of everyone in the organization, it is the direct responsibility of the key decision makers in general and the point person in particular. His or her job as a leader is to put flesh on what can often seem to be sparse, abstract ideas, so that they spring to life in a fresh way that has meaning and will impact the lives of those under the ministry.

The rest of this chapter presents seventeen practical values-casting methods that can be used by ministry leaders, particularly pastors, staff, and laypeople. These methods are practical because they help people understand values that otherwise would come across as just abstract ideas.

Keep in mind that leaders need to constantly communicate the core values, as well as the mission and vision, using as many methods as possible. Regular values casting affirms and reaffirms primary beliefs. When this does not take place, people begin to assume that the beliefs are not really important or that the leaders are no longer committed to them or that the beliefs may be changing. Also, people perceive and learn in different ways. That is why using multiple methods, as opposed to a single method, will prove more effective.

The Leader's Life

The leaders of any organization communicate its values by modeling the credo. Behavioral modeling is one of the most effective means for communicating a concept to people. Luke records that the early church "devoted themselves to" their values—an obvious reference to how they lived and went about their ministry. A leader who personifies the ministry's values accomplishes several important objectives.

The leadership modeling process is foundational to all the other methods for values casting. A church may be communicating its values in every way possible; however, if the leadership does not consistently live those values or in some way contradicts them, then those actions will nullify the effectiveness of the other methods. Conversely, a leader who lives his and the organization's values undergirds and promotes all the other methods for values communication.

The leader's actions will clearly demonstrate and reinforce the values that he or she believes to be important—the high-priority values. Every church organization has numerous beliefs, and the leader's behavior indicates which are the more important ones. This is why it is so crucial that the leader have ownership of the ministry's values set and be willing to commit to them. A lack of ownership means that the leader will follow a values set different from the organization's stated values. The result will be chaos, disruption, and the potential demise of the organization. This is what happened to Pastor David Johnson and Hope Community Church.

The leader's life translates the values into action. When leaders (staff, board, and others) consistently model the primary beliefs, people catch a glimpse of what the values look like when fleshed out in real-life ministry situations. They watch the leaders to see how the primary values affect a person's life, starting with the leaders' lives and spreading to their own lives. The leaders' behavior answers two questions: How is living these values affecting our leaders' ministry lifestyle? and, How will our living these primary beliefs make a difference in our lives and in our ministries?

The leader's behavior establishes the acceptable norms of behavior for the rest of the organization. Those on the ministry team know what is expected of them. They have a feel for where and when they might cross the line. They also know what to expect from a leader, such as a senior pastor. Should their values change, they know, as well, that they need to look for another ministry that shares common cause with their new values. Others in the organization know what is expected of them and have similar expectations of the leader. Consequently, behavior has a rippling effect from senior pastor to custodian.

The leader's life brings credibility to his or her values and ministry—especially in the church. The followers in an organization regularly observe its leadership for evidence of credibility. They ask, Is this person qualified, or still qualified, to lead us? Does this person really believe what he or she professes? In particular, people look to overt behavior as the chief indicator of values compliance. Here passion is critical. They want to know if the people they are following are passionate about the key beliefs. Living one's values is a foundational must; passionately living one's values builds a credibility superstructure. Should the leader lose that passion, however, it will take the edge off his or her credibility.

The Written Credo

Churches must articulate their values in a written statement or credo. Just as the leaders' lives are foundational to the other values-casting methods, so is the written credo. Until a values set is clear enough to be written on paper, it is not ready to be communicated through other means. Writing a credo provides a clear, communicable message. As we have seen, writing the credo necessitates defining and refining the beliefs with precision. Any logical flaws or inconsistencies are exposed and remedied during the process.

Leaders convey the values in a number of different, significant ways. This is difficult for some but easier for others. Men and women lead with different styles.[5] Many different methods of values casting can be used, but none of them will be effective if there is not a clearly written credo from which all the leaders in an organization are working.

The Leader's Message

Next, the leader's message casts the critical values. In a parachurch ministry, the message will take the form of a speech or sermon that the leader or key decision maker delivers to the ministry team. Certain parachurch ministries, such as Christian publishing houses and counseling ministries, rarely use this form. Communication takes place more through other methods, such as memos, newsletters, and house organs. They are missing, however, an ideal opportunity to convey both the vision and values in a group context. A certain dynamic is present when the leader casts the organization's vision and key values before an assembled group (see Nehemiah 8). The Amway organization and Mary Kay Cosmetics, as well as others, have discovered this, as evidenced by their yearly rallies. Why have Christian organizations missed the importance of collective communication?

In the church the message usually takes the form of a sermon that the pastor or someone on the pastoral team delivers on a Saturday evening or, more commonly, on a Sunday morning. The pulpit represents for people in many cultures a vital platform for leadership. The congregation looks at the person behind the pulpit as the leader of the church, whether or not this is true. Consequently, the sermon is a primary vehicle that the leadership uses to cast its beliefs and dreams.

The speaker in the parachurch context or the preacher in the church context should be a good communicator. To cast values poorly could have a negative effect. Gifted speakers motivate and catalyze their audiences to get behind the ministry's values and vision. They present the organizational values in such a way that they light a fire under their people. Poor communicators have the potential to defuse a significant values set. They have a way of putting out fires rather than igniting them.

Several key ingredients characterize the messages of able, articulate communicators. Pastors and other church leaders speak with good understanding. They know both their people—their needs, hopes, dreams, and aspirations—and their topic. They speak articulately. They are careful about the words they use. They may speak of "completely committed Christians" or "fully devoted disciples" or of developing "redemptive relationships." They speak positively, not negatively. You find out what they are for more than what they are against. They often speak with charisma. They are animated, expressive, even passionate about their topic. They are authentic. They are the same from core to crust; what you see is what you get. In particular, they believe what they are saying. You know it because they practice what they preach.

A danger is ever present for beliefs casters who are good speakers—specifically pastors of churches. Because they are such good speakers, they receive many accolades from their audiences for their communicative abilities. People may drive long distances to hear them speak. Consequently, these pastors view the sermon or message as the only vehicle for communicating the vision and values. Rather than using a variety of methods to regularly cast the church's DNA, they use only the sermon to cast the values a few times each year.

Formal and Informal Conversation

Conversation is an often overlooked method for communicating values. I divide conversation into formal and informal. Formal conversation is a type of official communication that takes place between the leadership and the followers in an organization. Some examples would be the announcements made from the pulpit on Sunday morning; while different preachers use different styles, it would certainly include the sermon (the conversational style); it would also include the prayers that take place on Sunday morning. An important question to ask is, What do you pray about in your church? Your prayers communicate your beliefs, whether or not you intend for them to do so.

Informal conversation takes place more frequently and is more important to values casting. You should ask, What do I and the people in my organization talk about during our leisure time? What is regularly on our minds? People discuss and communicate values over a hot cup of coffee at a local restaurant, while washing their cars in the driveway, while greeting one another in the hallway, when they drop their kids off at the church's nursery or a local day care, in a conversation over the phone, and so on. Pastors cast values informally when driving to the airport with their staff. They also cast values when they take time to pray with staff over the ministry.

You may find it valuable to pay attention to your formal and particularly to your informal conversations with people. Keep a mental diary of what you say over a couple of days or even a week. Ask yourself, What primary values do I communicate in my conversations with people? When I pray with people, what do I pray for? When I drive through

a neighborhood in the inner city or in suburbia, what do I talk about
with my staff?

Stories

The stories that people tell within and about their ministries clarify
and communicate their key beliefs. Like conversation, they take two
forms—formal and informal. Formal stories are the official claims of
the ministry. You read about them in a parachurch periodical or in the
church newsletter. They are found in public relations pieces that the
organization releases to the public, often through the press. They are
also contained in publications, such as Reformed Theological Seminary's
RTS Bulletin or Dallas Seminary's *Kindred Spirit*. Both contain articles
written by their alumni and stories about the schools and the influential
people related to the institutions. And both are circulated among their
constituencies.

The most effective stories, however, are informal. Alan Wilkins writes,
"My research in organizations suggests that many of the values that are
adopted as shared vision, as well as the conventions people learn, are
passed on through informal stories."[6] He explains:

> Stories of actual events inside the organization are often more credible
> than official claims because the person who is telling the story may not
> be a company official (with obvious pro-company biases) and because
> the story is concrete, unlike the abstract vision statements. In addition,
> stories give people a chance to improvise their own implementation of
> organization-sponsored values.[7]

Every church has within its culture a rich inventory of stories that
are told over and over from one generation to the next. These stories,
whether real or legendary, form a corporate memory that embodies the
group's values. In addition, they serve as a concrete means to communicate what otherwise might be general, abstract truths.

Wise leaders will capitalize on the stories of their ministries to communicate their beliefs; they will become storytellers. Those who lead
established ministries make a grave mistake if they ignore or neglect the
institution's stories, because they are an integral part of the ministry's
culture and they play a vital role in defining what the ministry is all
about. Leaders should collect and pass on the rich heritage of stories
that so warmly and ably communicate and illustrate the organization's
overriding precepts.

Those who lead new, entrepreneurial church plants must not ignore
the opportunities they have to create stories that others will use in

the future to cast key beliefs. An unusual and striking example from the marketplace is a story circulated about Seymour Cray of Cray Research. Each spring Cray, a sailing enthusiast, designs and builds a sailboat. However, at the end of a summer of sailing, he burns the boat so that next year's design will not be affected by it.[8] Whether the story is folklore or fact, it conveys the values of innovation and creativity to his people.

Alan Wilkins suggests that leaders pounce on these kinds of opportunities to cast values.[9] For example, if a core value of the church is evangelism, leaders will pounce on opportunities to share their faith with lost people. Then later they will tell their evangelism stories, which communicate to their people that "evangelism is important around here."

Programs

A subtle but authentic way that a corporation casts its values is through its program, its plan for achieving its goals. This applies specifically to the church. The ministries that actually take place in the church communicate its values, regardless of what the church says in any credo. In effect, what you see is what you get, whether positive or negative.

Programming is the litmus test of a ministry's beliefs and dream. The ministry's program measures what it believes it is doing and what it actually is doing. First, does it have a program? A church can profess to value prayer; it may have a carefully crafted statement in its credo about the value of prayer. However, if it does not program for prayer, then prayer is not a core value. An appeal for evangelism in a strong Bible-teaching church—without a program to implement it—or an appeal for more Bible teaching in a strongly evangelistic church—without a program—falls on deaf ears.

Even if a ministry has a program for the implementation of a value, it does not mean that the ministry owns the value. It's important to ask, Are people involved in the program? Traditionally, churches have set aside Wednesday evenings in their ministry programs for prayer. However, in the 1980s and 1990s, participants were scarce. This announces that the people may not value prayer, at least not on Wednesday nights. By way of contrast, Church on the Rock, formerly in Rockwall, Texas, a suburb of Dallas, has programmed prayer into its ministries. It set aside 5:00 on a weekday morning as a time for its prayer warriors to meet for intercessory prayer. The church reported that several hundred people were present. Many wore combat fatigues to communicate how important this prayer time was to the spiritual warfare of their church.

Visual Images

Visual images cast values. When explained, images or artifacts serve as visible reminders of the organization's beliefs. They are concrete objects that represent abstract values. They do not communicate the beliefs by themselves but serve to call attention to or remind people of values that have already been communicated by other methods. Whereas some methods appeal to the ears (as with a sermon), this one appeals to the eyes. It helps people "see" the values. There are several examples.

One is a PowerPoint or slide-tape presentation. This is a highly effective audiovisual technique that artfully blends a sound track, consisting of a song or prepared text, with a series of slides, which can focus on people, places, or events. At one time, I used a slide-tape presentation to communicate the value of world evangelism and outreach in a church-planting class that I teach at Dallas Seminary. The presentation included thirty to forty slides of lost people around the world and was accompanied by the contemporary Christian song "Jesus Saves."

Two problems exist with this method. The first is time. It may consume a significant amount of time to take and develop the photographs and coordinate them with the sound track. The other is money. Some cost is incurred in developing the slides and purchasing or renting the equipment. You will also need permission to use a contemporary music tape, and this will involve a charge. The benefits outweigh the disadvantages, however. Someone other than the primary leader, perhaps an adolescent with audiovisual talents, can minister to the organization in this area. Also, someone connected with the ministry may be willing to defray the costs or may loan you the equipment.

Another visual image is a well-designed logo. It has several advantages. If there are people in the church or ministry with graphic abilities, there will be little if any cost in designing and developing the logo. Most Christian bookstores provide clip-art materials that have sections with logos that can be used. Outside of the initial workup, the logo requires little time from the values caster. In addition, it requires little time of the viewer, usually only a glance, to catch the value.

You might develop a logo for your credo and place it on letterhead, memos, signs, newsletters, advertising, bulletins, vehicles, products, music slides, hymnals, equipment, identification cards, and so on. The genius of the logo is that it casts the values in multiple ways at the same time. A person could attend church, for example, and see the logo on the sign out front, in the bulletin, and on a music slide. He or she is exposed to the church's credo many times at one event.

Another visual image is a button or pin. In the past, various ministry organizations have affixed a fishhook or *ichthus* symbol to a lapel pin or button. They have used these symbols to catch the attention of lost persons and catalyze discussions about spiritual matters. My suggestion is that a ministry use the same approach to communicate a core value such as evangelism. People in the organization see the pin or button and it reminds them that evangelism is an important part of the ministry's bottom line.

Numerous media exist for presenting visual images of essential beliefs. Posters, pictures, paperweights, refrigerator magnets, sticky notes, coffee mugs, tee shirts, decals, bumper stickers, banners, and paper products (napkins) are among the many items that can be used.

Language and Metaphor

An organization's language and metaphors subtly or overtly convey its values. Churches are in the people business; that is, they work with and minister directly to people. How that ministry views people, therefore, is critical to the accomplishment of its vision. If two ushers in a church, for example, whisper to one another, "Here come those jerks!" when the doors first open, then no one should be surprised if people do not feel valued—they will be treated like jerks. In a school that depends on students for survival, someone may overhear a professor say to another, "If it weren't for students, this would be a great job!" Or they might hear him or her say, "I live to minister to and work with these students. Without them I would go somewhere else!"

Of particular importance is the use of metaphor. People use this language expression around us daily. They talk about "running" to the corner store—in their cars—"plowing" through a crowded corridor, or "sailing" through an assignment. In *The Leadership Challenge,* Kouzes and Posner describe the use of language and metaphor at Disney World, an organization that is also in the people business. For example, Disney has no employees, only "performers," who function as "hosts" and "hostesses." And their customers are "guests."[10] Perhaps the church would better communicate such values as the importance of people and friendliness if it referred to all of its people as "hosts" and "hostesses," or better, "servants," and to its visitors as "guests."

A Brochure

A well-designed brochure communicates the core values of a ministry. Over the past decade a significant number of visionary churches have realized the benefit of developing and producing brochures with information about their organization. This is vital in what is now a skeptical information age in which the public often demands prior knowledge before it will attend any Christian event, especially if it is church-related.

Over the years I have collected a number of brochures, most of which are from churches. The contents provide a wide range of information, such as the name, location, phone number, staff, and a map to help locate the building. Some develop brochures for new church starts. They usually answer three questions: Why are we planting this church? What kind of church will it be? How will we plant it? Established churches develop brochures that serve to attract new members and apprise potential members of the church's services.

I suggest that every ministry, church, and parachurch develop at least one brochure that communicates its DNA. My samples reveal that few churches, especially established ones, use brochures for this purpose. In most cases everything but their beliefs and dream is included. Some recently planted churches include a vision and even a mission statement, but only a few have an accompanying values statement. The values set that would appear in a brochure could be an abbreviated or full version of the credo. It would follow and support the vision statement.

Cassettes, CDs, and Videos

America is presently passing through the information age at breakneck speed. American marketplace guru Tom Peters recently mentioned that he could retreat to his farm situated in a quiet New England landscape and still maintain contact with the entire world. He has accomplished this with three items: a computer, a modem, and a fax machine.

While books are still in and will probably be so for many more years, cassettes, CDs, and videos have been valuable communication devices for a long time. For example, one company offers cassette tapes that summarize what the latest books are saying about leadership and management in the marketplace. One tremendous advantage is that they are so user-friendly. Simply pop the cassette or CD into a car's deck or view a video, and you have instant information.

No good reason exists for the visionary leader or organization not to use this technology to cast core values in a church or in a parachurch ministry. I have used an audiotape of a visionary sermon to help a core group in a recently planted church catch a vision for targeting and reaching unchurched non-Christians. I use videotapes in my classes at Dallas Seminary to communicate core values to students preparing for pastoral ministry. One video is of a seeker service at Willow Creek Community Church. The service conveys such values as the pursuit of excellence, lost people matter to God, and creativity and innovation are important in ministry.[11]

Celebrations and Heroes

The values that you celebrate and the people whom you present as heroes convey a clear values set. First, you must determine if you want to celebrate values. Contrary to Scripture, some Christians believe that it is wrong to celebrate. For others, it does not fit their unique style—a better reason. Some questions for those who do celebrate are, What do we celebrate in this congregation? If the ministry values evangelism, does it celebrate every time a person comes to faith? Certainly this is the case in heaven (Luke 15:7, 10); why not on earth (vv. 23–24)? Perhaps a spiritual birthday party would be appropriate. Kouzes and Posner wisely point out that celebrations are to the organization's culture what the movie is to the script or the concert is to the score. They express values that are difficult to express any other way.[12] However, problems arise when you attempt to celebrate beliefs that are not key to the ministry. Kouzes and Posner add, "Authenticity is what makes most conscious celebrations work."[13]

Most organizations have their heroes. Such people are important because their godly examples and servant ministries personalize and communicate the organization's core values. They also serve as values and vision role models for others in the organization. Most often they are the founders and early leaders in the ministry. The Old Testament celebrates numerous heroes, such as Abraham, Moses, Joshua, Caleb, Isaiah, Daniel, and Nehemiah. The New Testament also has its heroes, such as Paul, Peter, Barnabas, James, and others. At Dallas Seminary Dr. Lewis Sperry Chafer is the founder and a hero of sorts. His desire to see men and women accept the Savior and to understand and teach the Bible casts a vision for evangelism and excellence in expository preaching.

It is most important that the organization make heroes of those within the ministry who are modeling its key beliefs. Its heroes must include more than its founders or key decision makers. If it values creativity and innovation as does Lakeview Community Church (Cedar Hill, Texas), in appendix A, then it must make heroes out of its creative and innovative people. If it values the pursuit of excellence in its ministries, it must declare as heroes those who pursue and achieve a high degree of excellence.

Skits and Drama

Skits and drama represent a most effective method for communicating central beliefs. The church has known and practiced this art form for centuries. Moreover, both traditional and contemporary churches use it as a medium to communicate biblical truth.

The more traditional churches implemented drama throughout the twentieth century, using it primarily at Easter and Christmas and most often to focus on an Old or New Testament narrative such as the Christmas story. When they perform, the actors and actresses dress according to the culture of the original biblical story, and carpenters build the set to reflect the same. The problem is that these presentations take so much time and effort that people desire to perform them only once or twice a year.

Drama in general and skits in particular played an increasingly important role in many of the culturally relevant new paradigm churches of the late twentieth century and play an even greater role in the twenty-first-century church. Most of these churches produce skits of ten minutes or less that complement or set up the sermon. Some use them every week; others use them once a month. The skits are not limited to biblical narratives but focus on biblical concepts in both the Old and New Testaments.

The use of drama and skits has become so effective that churches desiring to exert a strong influence in the twenty-first century, as well as cast their values and vision, should consider using drama in their services. Skits require little financial outlay and do not place much strain on participants' time. People who have acting talents and abilities are usually found in even the smallest churches. This art form also provides a ministry opportunity for young people and has the potential to attract those in the arts community, many of whom are unchurched.

Most important, drama teams can use this art form to communicate the organization's highest-priority beliefs. Actually, if drama teams convey only the church's DNA, it would be worth the time and effort. While it may require little, if any, work from the professional staff, it provides a valid ministry outlet for those who may not have found a place of service anywhere else in the ministry organization. A good minidrama has the potential to capture people's attention in ways that the sermon cannot. Churches that overlook or ignore this art form sell themselves short in terms of casting their values before the people in today's audience.

The Newcomers' Class

An excellent format for conveying the values, mission, and dream is the newcomers' class. This concept applies either to a church or to a parachurch ministry. Most older, typical churches have conducted new members' classes since their conception. They cover a variety of topics ranging from the church's history to its constitution and bylaws.

Because of the large and growing unchurched Christian and non-Christian population, I would change the name of the class in a church context from New Members to Newcomers. Today's skeptical unchurched people are not interested in membership in a church. It calls for the kind of commitment that some are not ready to make.

The term *newcomer* is a softer, gentler term than *new member*. It conveys that a person, even an unchurched person, can come and check the class out without having to sign, stand, sing, or say anything. It attempts to honor people's desire to know more about the organization without all the trappings of a hard sell. If the church has a formal membership, the newcomers' class can explain what membership is all about and why the organization deems it important.

Regardless of what you call it, the newcomers' or new members' class provides an excellent opportunity to cast the church's values. It is a time when people either are curious about the church or are considering a stronger commitment to the ministry. They must know where the church is going (mission and vision) and what it is committed to (values) as well as how it will accomplish its direction (strategy). Such a class will eliminate some people and attract and encourage others.

Other Methods

Other means for casting the organization's essential beliefs exist. A talented cartoonist could develop a series that would appear in a bulletin, newsletter, or house organ. The pastor could give a state of the ministry message. Just as the president delivers a state of the Union address once a year, so the president of a ministry or the pastor of a church could deliver a state of the ministry message that assesses how well the ministry is accomplishing its stated values and vision.

The performance appraisal also conveys values. Every ministry, church and parachurch, should regularly evaluate its personnel. The key to this is the performance appraisal, and a major portion of the appraisal should assess commitment to core values. In doing so, it clearly articulates for all employees and ministry volunteers the critical ministry values.

A church would be wise to place its DNA in general and its values in particular on its web site. Many people, especially young people, will consult and use a church's web site to discover what it believes long before they will visit the church.

Methods for casting a ministry's values are numerous. I have touched only the tip of the communication iceberg in this chapter. The only limits to creating new methods and recovering old effective ones rest in the mind or the creative abilities of the visionary leader. Therefore, visionary leadership should periodically brainstorm and unleash people's creative abilities to come up with new, unique methods to communicate the values.

Practical Values-Casting Methods

The Leader's Life	Cassettes, CDs, and Videos
Written Credo	Celebrations
Message/Sermon	Heroes
Formal and Informal Conversation	Skits and Drama
Stories	Newcomers' Class
Programs	Cartoons
Visual Images	Performance Appraisal
Language and Metaphor	Ministry Web Site
A Brochure	

Questions for Reflection and Discussion

1. In your church who is responsible for casting the values? Does the point person cultivate, communicate, and clarify the core values? Do any others? If yes, identify them.
2. Does your ministry have a vision statement? Why or why not? Does it have a credo? Why or why not?
3. Do the people in your ministry comprehend its values? If your answer is yes, how do you know? Does the leadership model the organizational values? Why or why not? Do the people view the values casters as men and women of good character and integrity? Does your credo have content validity? Why or why not?
4. Who makes up your church's ministry community? Who makes up your ministry constituency? Why should you convey your values to the latter group?
5. If you are the primary leader or a major decision maker in your ministry, do you model the credo in your life? If yes, how do you know? Is there anyone in the organization who would tell you if you did not? Do you as a leader intentionally cast the core values through a speech or sermon? If so, how often? If you are a good communicator, do you rely primarily on the message or sermon to convey the values? If yes, what is the limitation of this approach?
6. How many methods does your church use to cast their core beliefs? Identify them. If several, does the ministry employ them at the same time? What methods listed in this chapter are you not using? Why not? Which unused methods would aid you in

values casting? Do you plan to adopt some or all of these methods? When?

7. Can you think of some other methods for conveying the organizational beliefs that are not mentioned in this chapter? What are they? What are some methods that other organizations in your community use to communicate their values? Would any of these methods help you?

6

WEAVING NEW VALUES INTO THE CONGREGATIONAL FABRIC
THE IMPLEMENTATION OF CORE VALUES

The black gumbo that makes up the soil of most yards in Dallas has proved a headache for homeowners who desire lush lawns during the scorching summer months of July and August. When it rains, the gumbo, which is heavily marbled with clay, absorbs only a little of the moisture before the rainwater runs off. This robs the St. Augustine and Bermuda grasses of much of the water they need to grow and spread. When it rains in the summertime, it is usually an intense, violent thunderstorm, but occasionally the grass gets a slow, soaking rain that allows the water to penetrate and mix deeply into the soil. This slow, soaking rain gets the moisture and nourishment all the way down to the roots of the grass, where it is needed most.

It is imperative that visionary churches cast their aspirational beliefs in such a way that they are more than just pleasant platitudes or words that sound great but have no bite. Ministries should accomplish more than just moving the values from paper to people; they must also take steps to make those values pervade the ministry. Like a slow, soaking summer rain, they must saturate the ground, penetrating to the very roots of the ministry.

115

Pastor David Johnson and the decision makers at Hope Community Church understand that communicating their values to their people is winning a major battle in the war. But to win the war, they must implement their new values so that they pervade the ministry. People need both to hear and to act—deeds must follow words. How do you implement the church's aspirational beliefs? How do you transform words into deeds? The answer is a four-step new values implementation process. It asks four core questions: Who is involved in values implementation? What are your ministry circumstances? How do you implement new values? How long will it take to implement these values?

The Personnel Involved

The first question—Who is involved in values implementation?—forces you to look at yourself and the people who make up the ministry. You, as a leader, are the one initiating change, and they are the ones who are most affected by the new values.

The Leader

The leader who seeks to implement new core values must first understand himself and how close a match there is between him and the people in the organization. The more they have in common, the better they will understand each other. When they share such things as where they grew up, ideas about rural versus urban issues, lifestyle, and education, the ability to implement the values will be heightened.

Have you been the leader or a leader in the ministry for a while, or are you coming in fresh from the outside? Is this a new work or an established ministry? Both questions focus on leadership credibility. Remember, followers grant the leader of a new work more credibility than they do in an established ministry. In a new work such as a church plant, they are joining him, whereas in an older ministry, he is joining them. I will say more about this below.

When a leader joins a ministry, as when a pastor accepts a call to an established church, according to C. Wayne Zunkel, he proceeds through three stages on his way to becoming a leader in the church. The first is the chaplain stage, which lasts from one to three years, when the pastor functions mostly as a chaplain, preaching and performing pastoral care but exercising limited influence as a leader. The second is the pastor stage, which lasts from three to five years, or it may last for the pastor's entire tenure at the church. During this time he gains more credibility and trust, as long as he leads with good character and competence. The last is the leader stage when the pastor becomes the recognized official as well as unofficial primary influencer of the church.[1] Here he has gained necessary credibility and trust from the people. One problem is that far too many pastors do not last long enough to become the leader. We discovered earlier that, according to George Barna, the average tenure for pastors in America is four years. The temptation is to become impatient with people and move on to a new ministry or drop out. Another problem is that some churches will not let a pastor lead regardless of how long he has been with the church.

The People

The leader who implements core values must also understand his people. Demographics and psychographics supply much helpful information. Most leaders who have been in a community for a while know and understand the organization's people. However, new leaders, especially those from outside the area, can greatly benefit from demographic and psychographic data.

Demographics provide information on the community such as age, sex, race, population, number and types of households, median income, level of education, occupation, and so on. Essentially, two sources for locating demographic information exist. Local sources are primary because they provide the most accurate and up-to-date information. They include public libraries, chambers of commerce, city and planning offices, zoning boards, realtors and real estate organizations, universities, colleges, public schools, utility companies, newspapers, commercial developers, and telephone surveys.

Psychographics help leaders discover why their people do what they do. In the marketplace, demographics aid a business in discovering who its customer is; psychographics help to discover why that customer buys. Psychographics describe a community's attitudes—how people feel about various issues. They also describe people's values—moral, organizational, and so on. And they reveal a community's lifestyle. For example, Claritas Corporation of Alexandria, Virginia, broke down Dallas County households into cluster groups based largely on lifestyle. The clusters were the Blue-Chip Blues Life, Young Influentials, the New Beginnings, Furs-and-Station Wagons, Golden Ponds, and the Shotguns-and-Pickups folk.[2]

To understand people, it also helps to examine the area in which the ministry is located—whether primarily urban or rural areas. The vast majority of people in the world today now live in the cities. In 1992 George Hunter wrote: "The United States population has moved from 20 percent urban in 1870, to 40 percent in 1900, to 70 percent by 1980, and will approach 90 percent urban in 2000 A.D."[3] This shift is redefining the lifestyles—and thus the values—of our world. Erwin McManus writes, "We stand at a crisis point in world history between a rural past and an urban future."[4]

The important application for the implementation of values is that urban areas are undergoing tremendous change and transition. Where change is taking place, it is much easier to implement new values and values forms. People in transition do not have the luxury of settling into a routine way of life for very long. To be effective, organizations have to regularly update the forms their values take. In a world of accelerating change, values forms will age quickly, requiring new, relevant forms if the values are to remain effective within the ministry.

Change is also taking place in most rural areas. Either people are abandoning these areas or nearby urban centers are expanding outward into them. In chapter 2 of *Unleashing the Church*, Frank Tillapaugh lists five differences between urban and rural communities.[5] These distinctions are presented in the chart below.

Rural and Urban Communities

Rural	Urban
Status quo	Change
Sameness	Diversity
Harmony	Conflict management
Smallness	Bigness
Established	Mobile

Even though rural areas are experiencing some change, the status quo still predominates. Values change very slowly if at all. In rural organizations such as churches, values tend to hang on for longer periods of time. This was the situation among the settlers (the old-timers) at Hope Community Church—but Pastor David Johnson did not know it. No one is in a hurry to change anything—much less the values and the forms they take. Leaders who attempt to implement new values in rural organizations do so at great risk to their credibility.

Ministry Circumstances

Ministry circumstances refers to the length of time the ministry has been in existence. Is it a new or an established ministry?

The New Ministry

In a new work such as a church plant, the leader's personal ministry values naturally become the ministry's core values. That is why it is so important that leaders discover their personal organizational core values and develop a personal credo before entering a ministry. It is mandatory for those in entrepreneurial ministries. The implementation of the core values involves communicating the founding leader's personal organizational values.

Church planting has certain advantages over ministry in an established church in terms of values. First, it is easier to lead people who come after you than those who were there before you. Chronological precedence seems to bestow a certain amount of territoriality and control. The early pioneers and settlers claim ownership of the virgin territory, and those who arrive later seem to intuitively know, accept, and respect this. In new ministries, people are joining you; you are not joining them. They automatically grant you up-front credibility as a leader. In an established ministry it is just the opposite. You are joining the pack, and therefore, you have to earn the right to lead. Your credibility is lower, and you have to gain people's confidence if you want to be their leader.

Also, new ministries usually attract people who are younger than you are. Because of your age and because you are already with the ministry, they will often grant you leadership credibility. In an established ministry it is the opposite; many of the people are older than you are, and you have to earn the right to lead them, which takes longer. People who come after and are younger than the leader tend to accept his or her values as a part of the leadership package. Values implementation becomes a more natural, easier process.

Initially, leaders of new ministries have fewer people problems, especially if they liberally communicate their congregational DNA up front. People who are interested in the ministry hear its focus (mission and vision) and understand what drives it (values). If they do not find common cause, either they move on or in time the leader encourages them to move on to another ministry that has more in common with them.

The Established Ministry

Implementing vital values in an established ministry can be more difficult than in a new ministry. It concerns pouring new wine into old wineskins. The majority of the people should have ownership of the present values, or they are not shared values. The problems begin when you attempt to introduce and implement new values in the ministry. For example, a pastor may discover that the church does not have a

Great Commission vision. He attempts to move the church toward a more evangelistic approach, hoping that people will embrace evangelism as a core value. Most likely, he will be greeted with such objections as, "We've never done it that way before!" "We tried that before and it didn't work!" People in established organizations are highly resistant to change. There are at least eight reasons for this.

1. Often people do not feel or sense a need to change. If you asked them to present a list of their felt needs, change would not be among them. When you attempt to introduce aspirational values, they are not responsive because they think all is well with the organization. Your job as a leader is to help these people see the need for adopting the new values. It is said that you can lead a horse to water, but you can't make it drink. But you can mix a little salt in with its oats.

2. Another reason change is difficult is that many people, especially in churches, prefer the status quo. They are like an infant who might, if it were possible, refuse to be born into this world, preferring instead the comfort and safety of his or her mother's womb. To move out of one's comfort zone and adopt new values is to risk giving up control and feeling vulnerable. It is only for brave souls. The wise leader will challenge people to stop looking at what is and to begin asking, What should be? and What can be?

3. People struggle with change because of vested interests. People who commit to an organization and its ministry accrue certain benefits such as power and position. An example is a position on a deacon or elder board in a church. As the organization grows, the power and prestige expand with it. An individual gains a greater say in what goes on. To adopt new core values, such as hiring the next pastor to be the leader of leaders, however, could mean the loss of all or much of that accrued power, prestige, and position within the organization.

4. If people do not trust those who would lead them through change, they will resist that change. The message here is clear. Any leaders in an organization will need sufficient credibility with their people before they can introduce new organizational values. In effect, followers are asking two questions of their leaders: Can you be trusted? and Do you know where you are going? Godly character and integrity are needed to answer the first question, and a clear, significant vision is the answer to the second.

5. People have a tendency to grant to old values and traditions a sacred quality that is not realistic. Over time these become organizational sacred cows that are immune to change. They are sacrosanct. Examples in the church may be the style of worship, an accepted version of the Bible, and Wednesday evening prayer meetings. Leaders must use clear

expository Bible teaching that distinguishes between biblical values and cultural forms that express those values.

6. One of the by-products of good leadership that implements new values is organizational growth and increasing complexity. People tend to resist the complex, however, opting instead for that which is simple. The result then is the stifling of good leadership and the maintenance of old, tired values. The solution is not to maintain the status quo but to balance good management with good leadership. Leaders catalyze change; managers program that change and bring order out of the complexity.

7. The paradigm effect also makes change difficult. A paradigm is a particular, shared mind-set, viewpoint, set of assumptions, or beliefs about reality or how things are. Joel Arthur Barker explains: "What may be perfectly visible, perfectly obvious, to persons with one paradigm may be quite literally invisible to persons with a different paradigm."[6] Thus a conflict of values exists.

8. Another reason for difficulty is self-centeredness. The reality is that some people are looking out for themselves. This is not new—Ananias and Sapphira in Acts 5 and the widows' dispute in Acts 6 are just two of many biblical examples. The problem is that few will admit to this. The solution is for the leadership to confront and deal with it as Peter did in Acts 5:3–4 and as the Twelve did in Acts 6:2–6.

Reasons for Resisting Change

Lack of need
Status quo
Vested interests
Distrust of leaders
Sacrosanct traditions
Complexity of change
Conflict of values
Self-centeredness

Implementing New Values

The task of values implementation is to incorporate the new values into older ministries. What can pastors and leadership teams do to help their established congregations own new values at their core? The answer is twofold: New values are both taught and caught.

New Values Are Taught

Values are taught, so teach them. It is imperative that churches teach their aspirational values. The obvious way to teach values in the church is through preaching in the worship services. I encourage all preachers to preach about the church's DNA (that includes its values) at least once a year. Another way is to use teaching contexts, such as a Sunday school class or an Adult Bible Fellowship (ABF). The church could coordinate the Sunday school or ABF teaching with that of the sermon. The sermon would present and review the values, and the congregation would discuss them in the Sunday school or ABF context.

Another excellent opportunity is a new members' or newcomers' class. Some churches do not believe in membership. One such church once told me they did not have a membership because they could not find it in the Bible. My response is that if we have to find all our practices in the Bible, it would eliminate about 95 percent of what we do in our churches. This is a bad hermeneutic (see my book *Doing Church*[7]). Just because something is not found in the Bible does not mean that it is wrong or that the early churches did not do it. I encourage churches to have a membership, because it encourages mental, emotional, and spiritual commitment to the church. A new members' class is a good time to communicate to people what the church deems important and an opportune time to cover the church's DNA, which includes its core values, and in this context, its aspirational values. Often a newcomers' class is directed toward those who may be interested in the church but not in membership. Regardless of their intentions, this is another opportunity to teach new values.

New Values Are Caught

New values are also caught, so help your people in every way possible to catch them. Often when we want a congregation to embrace something new, we tend to focus solely on preaching and teaching the concept. At least this is what first comes to the pastor's mind. He says to himself, *If I want people to get this new idea or value, I must preach or teach it.* Perhaps a more effective approach is to help them catch new ideas. Values catching is a subtle but most effective way to create ownership of new values. The following are several vehicles that aid you in this process.

MODELING

The first vehicle is modeling the new values. Every church has numerous values, some of which are more important than others. The way leaders live simply reinforces what they believe is important, regardless of what they say. And they must realize that people are watching how they live 24-7. Contrary to much of the twentieth century, people—especially younger ones—in the twenty-first century are more critical of their leaders. People have seen too many leaders fall morally or fail to keep their promises, and they will not blindly follow them. They will observe their leaders carefully and follow those who prove credible over time. Thus leaders' words *teach* their values, but their lives help their people *catch* their values. And the latter affirms the former.

Visiting

Another method is visiting churches that model new values. Some people catch a vision better by visiting a ministry that has the same vision that the leadership wants to own. So leaders will determine their ministry's vision and then find a ministry in the area with the same or approximate vision. Next, they will take as many of their people as possible to visit that ministry. The response often is, "Now we see what you are talking about."

The same works for aspirational values. Find a church that already values and lives what you want your church to live and value, and take your people for a visit. I am aware of a number of churches in Dallas, Texas, that have taken their people to a Willow Creek Community Church conference or one of Willow Creek's evangelism conferences. When they return, they practically own evangelism as a core value, because they have seen and felt what it is like for unchurched seekers to come to faith in Christ.

Enculturating

In *Beyond Entrepreneurship,* Collins and Lazier define *enculturating* as "instilling and reinforcing the vision, especially the core values." They explain, "You can't assume that people fully understand the precepts of your organization when they walk in the door. You need to educate them. And you need to educate them *early.*"[8]

Collins and Lazier suggest several methods used in the marketplace that facilitate the enculturation process. One is to use a starter kit. It consists of written materials, including the DNA (mission, vision, strategy). A ministry could employ a ministry starter kit or a church could call it a new member's kit.

Also, Collins and Lazier suggest that the leader write a letter or article a few times a year that touches on the core values and includes stories of how employees, members, or staff fleshed out the beliefs in unusual, creative ways. Circulate the letter among your people or publish it in an employee or ministry newsletter.

Writing the history of the company or church is another way to enculturate. Give a copy to every new employee or member and encourage or insist that he or she read it. Deliver a corporate philosophy-of-ministry talk to all new people or employees. Assign each new person a buddy who takes him or her under the wing and educates that person in the organization's values.[9]

TRAINING

After the organization has enculturated the new member or employee, a need arises for some initial training for the specific job or ministry he or she will perform. This training can be used to further implement the values.

A core value in many new paradigm churches is lay ministry. The values slogan is "Every member a minister." That means that one of the expectations that a church has for its members is involvement in ministry. To implement such a value requires a lay mobilization or training process. The process by itself imparts the lay-ministry value. It can be used to impart the other values as well.

Church and parachurch ministries can use a variety of training methods that will prepare people for their individual responsibilities in the ministry. Undergirding this training are the basic values of the organization. Some training methods are written manuals, videotaped and audiotaped programs, and an internship or apprentice program. You may want to use other organizations for training in specific skills. Some marketplace corporations have developed their own training "universities." Most have heard of McDonald's Hamburger University. But there is also Apple University and Precision Lenscrafters University.[10] Not to be left behind, Lakepoint Baptist Church, located in Rockwall, Texas, a suburb of Dallas, has developed Lakepoint University, which meets to train church leaders and members quarterly on Saturday mornings.

PROMOTING

Most ministry organizations promote their people in some way. Churches often promote qualified, gifted lay followers to lay leadership positions. Some of the megachurches recruit their professional staff personnel from their lay leadership. Willow Creek Community Church brought Lee Strobel on as a teaching pastor. He was not a seminary graduate but a layman who accepted Christ through the ministry of the church and was trained under its ministry.

An organization can use the promotion to help people catch the fundamental ministry beliefs. The practice is simple. Those who demonstrate job or ministry expertise as well as ownership of and faithfulness to what the organization is all about—the values—are promoted.

Those who do not are not promoted. Promotions reflect the strength of the individual's commitment to the ministry's DNA. Consequently, the people who move up in the organization hold to its bottom-line beliefs, and the values are not compromised or dissipated.

REWARDING

Rewards for values commitments will help congregants catch the values undergirding those commitments. The key is to make sure that those who commit to and live the organizational values are the most rewarded and most satisfied people in the ministry.

Scripture teaches not only that those who place their faith in Christ will go to heaven in the future life, but that God will reward them for service in this life. In 1 Corinthians 3:10–15 Paul teaches that God will judge the quality of every Christian's work with fire. And he will reward all that survives. If God chooses to reward the quality works of his committed people, should not the ministry organization follow suit? Rewards send a clear, tangible message to people about what's important. It is true that what is rewarded gets done.[11] However, it must get done in a way that brings significance, satisfaction, and enjoyment to the doer and honors and pleases God. Financial reward alone is insufficient. Leaders in Christian ministries must be aware of this fact. Most Christian organizations are nonprofit and tend to pay lower salaries to their professionals than the marketplace does. Also, ministries depend heavily on volunteer support. Consequently, Christian leaders need to come up with ways, other than salaries, to reward their people.

There are two kinds of rewards: formal and informal. Formal rewards are expected in many situations and consist of such things as promotions, raises, bonuses, and so on. Informal rewards are not expected and can make the difference in people's commitment to God and to the ministry. They consist of such things as verbal or written praise, a thank-you note, a smile, a word of congratulations, a pat on the back, overheard bragging, being used as a positive ministry example (a hero), a certificate, or a wall plaque.

STORYTELLING

Stories illustrate new values and communicate them in concrete ways. People love stories. In fact, storytelling has been a universal means of communication throughout history and across cultures. I encourage your church's leadership to look for and repeatedly tell stories that illustrate aspirational values. They must regularly cast them in formal and informal situations as well. Though a church may not actually value evangelism, every church knows of a situation in which someone came to faith, likely in a dramatic way. This may have happened in the past or just recently. Regardless, capture and savor these stories and tell them formally and informally every opportunity you have.

EVALUATING

I have observed in various contexts, both church and parachurch, that whatever gets evaluated gets done. It is my view that though few people like to be evaluated, evaluation helps people improve their performance. Because I am a tenured faculty person at Dallas Seminary, my students are required to evaluate me only every three years. My practice, however, is to have them evaluate me every semester. Is this because I enjoy being evaluated? Hardly. It is because I want to get better at what I do.

I also realize that what gets evaluated gets done. When my classes evaluate me every three years, they use a form provided by the seminary. We as a faculty and administration have decided what we believe is important, and we have placed it in that evaluation form. Since all of the faculty know what is on that form, we pay close attention to it and seek to accomplish in our classes the things it evaluates. I believe that the church should follow suit. Not only will churches get better at being the church, but people will catch and embrace new beliefs.

How Long Will It Take?

We must remember that adopting new values immerses us in the change process. We are asking people to do something that is for most of us very difficult—to change. And changing our values is doubly difficult.

Ken Blanchard believes that to help people through change, it is important to be aware of the four distinct levels of change. One is the knowledge level. It is the easiest level, when people learn something new based on a tape or something read or heard. This involves the teaching of new values. The second level is attitude. This is when you know something and feel strongly about it. Attitude is harder to change because it involves the emotions. The third level is behavior. Behavior is even more difficult to change because you have to overcome or eliminate an old way of behaving and implement a new one. The fourth and most difficult level is organizational change. Blanchard says that it takes three to five years to accomplish a major change in an institution. He argues, for example, that it is much easier to plant a church than to revitalize one.[12]

In their book *Managing by Values*, Ken Blanchard and Michael O'Connor state no less than four times that it takes two to three years for values to change.[13] Time looms as a major factor in organizational change. In *Executive Success: Making It in Management*, Eliza Collins argues that easing a large organization into a major shift of values takes anywhere from three to eight years.[14] My point in citing these writers is that change takes time. What often happens is that a group of leaders adopts several aspirational values and anxiously attempts to implement them. However, when people do not respond right away, the leaders become discouraged and assume they have failed in their implementation efforts. Where they may fail, if at all, is showing the patience that is necessary for a group to take on new values as actual values.

Questions for Reflection and Discussion

1. How close a match are you and the people in the ministry? What do you have in common with them? Do you share such things as where you grew up, ideas about rural versus urban issues, lifestyle, and education?
2. Are you involved in a new or an established ministry? How hard is it to implement organizational core values in a new ministry? Why? How hard is it to implement values in an established ministry? Why?
3. Assuming your ministry is a church, take the Readiness for Change Inventory, appendix E. What are the chances that change can take place in your ministry?
4. Why might a leader such as a pastor attempt to implement new values in an established ministry? Give several reasons why people resist change. Do these reasons make sense? Of the eight reasons given why people resist change, how many are true of you and/or the people in your ministry? Did any other reasons for change resistance come to your mind while reading this section? If yes, what are they?
5. What does the fact that there seem to be more ways to catch values than to teach them tell you? What are some of the vehicles for values implementation that you believe would work for your church? Why? What would not work? Why? Can you think of any other vehicles not mentioned here?
6. How long do you think it will take for people in your church to "buy in" to new values? Why? What does this teach you about patience? Does your ministry have enough time to wait for change? If not, what could you do?

7

HOW NOT TO DROP THE BALL
THE PRESERVATION OF CORE VALUES

Anyone who has flown a few times in an airplane has experienced this familiar scenario. The big jet quickly lifts off the runway, noses upward, and rapidly climbs to its designated altitude with both the No Smoking and Fasten Seat Belt signs brightly lit. When the plane arrives at the proper, assigned altitude, the captain makes a few announcements and then turns the signs off, allowing the passengers to walk around the cabin if necessary. Somewhere between takeoff and landing, however, the plane begins to shake, jerk, and bounce in midair as if some invisible hand of a giant baby boy clutches it and is playing with it as though it were a toy. The signs go back on, the pilot announces that the plane is not in serious jeopardy but is passing through some turbulence due to weather, and he asks that the passengers stay seated for the present.

Flying in an airplane has much in common with leading an organization. There are times when the ministry glides along smoothly without a hitch and times when it experiences some turbulence. When leaders fly through ministry turbulence, they must tightly fasten their seat belts. The seat belts in ministry organizations are the convictions that you determine for yourself—those things about you and your ministry that must not change. They consist of such things as your vision, doctrinal beliefs, and most important, your core organizational values.

Pastor David Johnson is excited. He has planted a church, and it has grown to around two hundred people in a year's time. Hope Community Church is excited too. It has called a new pastor, an older man who has lived in the community for years, and the church shows signs of springing back to life. A number of older people from the community have returned, and some new faces are present as well. It is only a matter of time, though, before both ministries will fly through some turbulence. Just as weather turbulence is a part of flying in an airplane, so organizational turbulence is a part of leading a ministry. The problem is that organizational turbulence can exact a heavy toll on core values and vision. How should Pastor David and the leaders at Hope Church respond in times of turbulence?

I have defined organizational values as the constant, passionate, sacred core beliefs that drive the ministry. The first word in the definition is the term *constant*. Once leaders have passed through a values formation period, such as takes place in their training, the beliefs that make up their personal and organizational credo should not change appreciably. This means that while the corporation is implementing its core values, it must also work hard at protecting and preserving them. Values preservation is essential to the life of the ministry. The core organizational values are to the ministry what the navigation system is to the plane, especially in times of bad weather when visibility is severely limited. These values guide leaders and keep them on course when the turbulence obscures the vision.

But what is involved in values preservation? What can leaders do to protect and preserve their values? What is to prevent them from dropping the ministry ball? Before answering these questions, we must first examine and understand the problem. Values preservation is the solution to the problem. But what is the problem?

The Problem

Every ministry encounters organizational turbulence. Most often it comes in the form of interpersonal conflicts. I suspect that when David Johnson begins to encounter some turbulence in his church plant, his estimation will sound something like the following: "The church is doing fine. Our attendance continues to climb, people are accepting Christ, and the services and care groups are running smoothly. However, the struggle for us is the interpersonal conflicts that have raised their ugly heads over the past month and a half. We just had our first annual meeting, and some people wanted to change a key part of the values and vision statement. All the phone calling that took place almost wore me out. There was politicking behind the scenes that I didn't know about. In addition, significant debate was taking place before and after the meeting over the DNA. I'm tired and emotionally empty.

"That's not all. Last fall a group of people from a defunct church in the area came and joined with our group. While we've assimilated some in the church, four or five families haven't made the transition. They've begun to grumble loudly that we aren't catering to their needs. Last night one couple had me over to their house so they could tell me all that they did not like about the church. They and some of the others probably won't stick, and that's okay. It's not that I don't care about these people; it's just that they want things to be just as they were in their old, now dead, church. But I'm not going to let that happen here."

Obviously the problem is the possible erosion of the ministry's vital organizational values as well as erosion of the mission and vision. Organizational turbulence poses the potential for values erosion. But how does such erosion happen and who are the culprits?

The Values-Erosion Process

Pastor David's ministry is facing the potential for values erosion. The process begins with conflict, usually interpersonal conflict, that leads to compromise.

CONFLICT

Interpersonal conflict is a fact of life for any organization, whether a church or any other ministry. Because people have different interests and needs and because they have differing backgrounds that lead to different values, conflict is inevitable. It is only a matter of time—you can count on it.

It happened to the early church in the first century. In Acts 4:32 Luke notes that in the church at Jerusalem, "all the believers were one in heart and mind." There was little interpersonal conflict. But not for long. Perhaps key to the lack of initial conflict was the believers' willingness to share their possessions with those who had material needs. This very situation, though good, led to an abuse that introduced conflict to the congregation. Ananias, apparently a member of the church, sold some property but kept back part of the money while indicating that he had given it all, perhaps to impress some of the people or to maneuver into a leadership position (5:1–2). Through Peter, God dealt with Ananias and ultimately took his life, thus ending the first conflict in the church (vv. 3–5).

The next conflict is the one in Acts 6:1–7 when the Grecian Jewish widows were being overlooked in the daily distribution of food. The leadership, the Twelve, resolved the conflict by choosing seven spiritually qualified men to take charge of the food distribution ministry. They made the decision based on organizational core values. The Twelve had to determine where they would spend their time in ministry. Based on their priority of values, they chose the ministry of the Word and prayer over the ministry of food distribution (vv. 2–3).

If interpersonal conflict happened in the church of the first century, it will happen in the church of the twenty-first century. I do not know of any ministry organization that has not experienced conflict. The key is how the leadership responds to the turbulence. They have a choice. They can respond in such a way that they protect and preserve the values and vision, as Peter and the Twelve did, or they can respond so as to erode and ultimately undermine and negate them. The latter response is one of compromise.

COMPROMISE

The popular prescription for conflict in far too many ministry quarters today is compromise. Many church boards that consist of laypeople believe that their primary job, besides making decisions affecting the ministry, is to keep the peace. When conflict erupts in the church, they quickly sue for peace, which usually comes in the form of compromise. They believe that compromise leads to congregational consensus.

This concept, however, is seriously flawed. While compromise may under some circumstances lead to consensus, it is a false consensus. True consensus takes place when the various parties in a conflict agree to disagree. They approach a conflict with the attitude that, because their views will be given a fair hearing, they will attempt to support the decision of the group, even if they disagree with that decision. A true consensus over values is better than fragmented support of those values. On issues, however, where opinions are extremely diverse and the stakes are high, compromise does not create true consensus; it creates concession and more compromise.

The leadership cannot afford to compromise the core organizational values of the ministry. Compromise and concession serve, in the long term, only to bargain away the organization's vital values. If those beliefs are to drive the ministry, they can never be compromised. Repeated compromise and concession by the organization's leaders broadcast to the ministry's constituency that the core beliefs are not really that important—any old value can drive this organization. And no one takes the corporation's values seriously.

Not only does compromise send a bad message, it diminishes the decision makers' ability to lead. When leaders gamble with a ministry's driving values, the stakes are high. Compromise and concession assure that all the players will lose big, and ultimately everyone will leave with empty pockets. Consequently, leaders must be able to identify conflicts that involve the ministry's core values and quickly and strongly confront them. This can only happen when all the leaders share a strong personal commitment to the credo and are not willing to concede parts of it no matter how major the conflict that may ensue.

INSTITUTIONALIZATION

Another way that values erode is through ministry institutionalization. Values erode as a result of years of ad hoc policies and ministry practices that have become institutionalized and thus have obscured the church's central values. How does this happen? A pastor may plant a church that values evangelism and solid Bible teaching. To flesh these out, the church develops various ministries and programs. In time the pastor may move on to plant another church. The problem is that the congregation has forgotten the values, because the people see only the programs and practices that are in place that promote and facilitate the values. In time the practices overshadow the values, and the latter are forgotten. If the practices are not regularly updated, they grow brittle and die, and the values may die along with them.

The Values-Erosion People

The people who contribute to values erosion are found both outside and inside the ministry organization. Nehemiah discovered this when Israel's unbelieving enemies, Sanballat, Tobiah, and Geshem, attacked his vision from without (Neh. 2:19; 4:1–8). But others attacked from within (6:10–13). You expect opposition from unbelievers and even some believers from the outside. However, unreasonable, misguided opposition from people within the ministry causes the most damage spiritually and emotionally to the leader. I call these people values vampires and values vultures.

VALUES AND VISION VAMPIRES

Values vampires are people who from within the organization either intentionally or unintentionally attempt to suck the lifeblood from the core values. Those who attempt the same with the vision are vision vampires. Some have a proclivity for both.

Values vampires, like vision vampires, are often well-intentioned congregants or workers who believe that they are practically defending the faith by opposing the organization's values and the means by which those values are expressed. In the church they are particularly concerned with contemporary worship styles, especially those that use such instruments as guitars and drums. They want things to be just like they were in their old, more traditional churches, and they long for a return to the good old days. While they view themselves as courageous defenders of the ministry, they are actually courageous defenders of the status quo, which is Latin for the mess we are in.

Values vampires will come out of their corners fighting because they believe that the leadership has made a major mistake—they have bought into the wrong values and values forms. Values vampires have convinced themselves that they are fighting for the faith. They are more than willing to verbalize all this to the leaders, and they spread the word to all those who will listen. They seldom seek compromise, preferring that the church change its values and adopt theirs.

Many are strong-willed people who exert an influence far out of proportion to their numbers. If you listened to them, you would believe that the entire church was upset about the credo. I refer to them as the organization's squeaky wheels. They have learned through practice that if you complain loud enough and often enough, most church boards will give you what you want simply to keep the peace. Rather than defending the faith, values and vision vampires are causing damage to the faith by eroding the values.

VALUES AND VISION VULTURES

Values vultures are similar to values vampires but have turned the temperature down a few degrees in that they aren't as intense. They could be vision vultures as well. They attack the values not by sucking the life out of them but by attempting over a lengthy period of time to pick them apart—they are perpetual nitpickers. They do not see themselves as crusaders or defenders of the faith. They are not so sure that the values are even against the faith. Their problem is that they simply do not vote for change. Like the vampires, their motto is "Come weal or come woe our status is quo."

In the typical church, values vultures have become accustomed to sitting in unofficially reserved places in pews, passing an offering plate, listening to organ music and to long, loud sermons. If the sermon does not last a minimum of forty-five minutes and the pastor does not perspire and get red in the face, they feel cheated—the man hasn't preached! These people have hired the pastor to do the work of the ministry. Their part is to be faithful to the church, which interpreted means showing up at all the meetings (Sunday morning and evening and Wednesday evening prayer meeting), dropping a check in the offering plate, and occasionally making an altar call. They know no other way; this is the way they have always done it, and they are not about to change now. They have adopted some questionable values and some unbiblical values. Leaders who attempt to introduce and implement new, biblical values, such as evangelism, Bible doctrine, or a mobilized laity, are greeted with a cold stare. Values vultures are a quiet but vocal minority, consisting primarily of the Builder generation, with a few Baby Boomers sprinkled in, who attempt to exert an influence that is far out of proportion to their actual numbers.

The Solution

The solution to the problem of values erosion is values protection and preservation, but that takes us back to the original questions: What is involved in preserving organizational values? and What can leaders do to protect and preserve the church's critical, biblical core values? My studies reveal that leaders and their ministries can implement some general and specific practices that will preserve those values and retard their erosion.

General Values Preservation

There are two practices that protect primary beliefs. One is values modeling and refers to the leader's life. The other is values casting and refers to the communication of the essential beliefs.

VALUES MODELING

As we learned in chapter 6 and other previous chapters, the point person—the primary leader of the organization—and the other key decision makers and influencers on the team must have a strong personal commitment to the organizational core values. If the primary leader is not sure, vacillates, or seems insincere, he will experience a credibility gap and the followers will not take the values seriously. Pastors and lay teams who have made a strong commitment to the values will have them uppermost in their minds. They will ask, How can I reinforce our beliefs through my example? How can I explain what I decide and do in terms of our values?

This is values modeling. The leadership must live and breathe the values. This does not require a charismatic personality as some suppose, although most leaders will be passionate about their beliefs. Instead, their personal commitment and example in making

and implementing decisions and in formal and informal contacts all
serve to preserve the values. The leaders' way of life, their patterns
of behavior, how they decide issues both big and small are reflec-
tive of their vital beliefs. Leaders who are consistent in these areas
engender and enhance the respect and admiration of their followers
and sometimes their detractors.

Perhaps the supreme test and opportunity for leaders to live their
key values is when the force of daily realities pressures them to compromise those beliefs. Daily realities both big and small are a threat to
organizational values. An example from the marketplace cited earlier
was the Tylenol episode. Several years ago, in response to product tampering, Johnson and Johnson voluntarily took Tylenol capsules off the
shelf—at a cost of more than one hundred million dollars. The actions
of Johnson and Johnson's leadership clearly and forcefully defended
and affirmed the central value that the company's first responsibility is
to their customers.

VALUES CASTING

Another general method for keeping the values before the people
and thus preserving them is the constant casting and recasting of
those values. Regularly exposing those who make up the ministry
organization (the ministry community) and those who have expressed
interest (the ministry constituency) to the bottom-line beliefs constantly removes the rust that collects on unused, unrealized values
and places over them a fresh coat of protective paint.

When many pastors hear the term *values casting,* they automatically
think of preaching. What better way to communicate the values than to
talk about them before a group of people? A pastor can stand in the pulpit
on Sunday morning and preach about the church's critical core values
until everyone understands and, hopefully, embraces them. What these
leaders and their organizations must realize is that there are numerous
ways to cast—communicate—the values in the organization. Preaching
and speaking is one of them, and it is an excellent method, provided
the values caster is an articulate communicator. But the ministry is in
trouble if it is depending only on communicating the values from the
lectern or pulpit and its values caster is not a good speaker. Regardless,
any ministry organization is most effective in values casting when it uses
a combination of methods at the same time. Chapter 5 recommends a
number of methods for accomplishing this goal. Some of those methods
involve the leaders' lives, the leaders' messages, a written values statement (credo), formal and informal conversations, storytelling, ministry
programs, visual images such as PowerPoint presentations or slide-tape
productions and logos, language and metaphors, a well-done ministry

brochure, cassettes, CDs, and videotapes, celebrations, values heroes, skits and drama, a newcomers' class, web site postings, and so on. The methods that are available to the values communicator are limited only by his or her imagination and creativity.

Specific Values Preservation

General values preservation utilizes values modeling and values casting so that organizations can prevent the erosion of vital beliefs under most circumstances. Specific values preservation focuses on specific situations and attempts to preserve values through prevention and correction.

PREVENTION

Values preservation through prevention attempts to implement certain processes that prevent values erosion. The concept is found in medicine. Health care professionals have learned that there are certain precautions a patient can take to prohibit disease and infection. Local health agencies will inoculate children to prevent them from catching smallpox, tetanus, typhoid, and a whole host of harmful, life-threatening diseases. Dentists insist that their patients floss and brush their teeth daily to limit tooth decay and possible gum infections.

In the same way, leaders and their organizations can put into place certain practices and programs that will preserve their most cherished beliefs. I will present two and remind you of others.

Recruiting. A church or parachurch corporation can preserve its core beliefs by attracting people, both leaders and followers, with similar beliefs. One way to accomplish this is to use the values to recruit people for their ministries. Christian Associates International is a missions organization that has targeted Europe for the planting of new, high-impact churches. Their strategy is to start English-speaking churches that attract English-speaking internationals. Linus Morris, the director, has discovered that with this approach, the new church can be up and under way in a relatively short period of time. That, however, is only phase one. Phase two is when the international church targets the nationals of the country it is in, using as a core the internationals reached in phase one.

While phase two may take a little longer than phase one, phase one provides the critical mass necessary to implement phase two. The values of the mission are team ministry; evangelism; contemporary worship; strong, relevant Bible preaching; and authentic community through small groups. These values and the forms they take, along with the unique strategy, have served to attract a number of like-minded young people to involvement with the mission.

Some churches tell the same story. A contemporary, new paradigm church in Dallas that strongly values worship and people has attracted a constituency with the same values. This church has used a contemporary worship form to capture authentic worship. They believe that people matter to God, and they have attracted a contingent of people who do not feel welcome or comfortable in other churches. People know and understand the values and recruit others to the ministry by word of mouth.

Jim Collins goes so far as to say that you cannot instill new values in people. He argues that you must hire those who already share your values. He writes, "Instead, the task is to *find* people who are already predisposed to sharing your core values."[1] Though I disagree with the idea that you can't instill new values, Collins makes the point that it is important to seek people who have values congruent with those of the church.

Enfolding. Enfolding is the process of bringing someone into the organization. It is the process of membership in a church; it is the process of hiring staff or recruiting volunteers for service in a church or in a parachurch ministry.

Enfolding is another excellent way to protect an organization's values. When a person desires to join a church, that church should have a newcomers' process in place that introduces the newcomer to the vision, strategy, doctrine, and critical core values of the church. At the very least, general agreement with these, especially with the church's DNA, is necessary before the church brings the individual on board. This may seem a little harsh, especially at a time in the history of the local church when membership is down. However, I believe that to bring a new person into an organization with which he or she does not share the values, mission, and vision does harm to both parties. Over time the individual will become dissatisfied with the church, and he or she will either attempt to change the DNA or leave. At the same time the church will become dissatisfied with the individual. The church would do the person a service by pointing him or her early on to another ministry in the community that shares similar values.

When a ministry hires staff or employees, the enfolding process can protect the organization's values. The employment interview process must identify people who have not only the right skills, education, and experience for the position but also the right beliefs. Ministries get themselves into trouble when they do not invest properly in the hiring process. The important questions are: Is this person a values fit? Does he or she buy into what we are all about? If his or her critical values do not align with those of the organization, the leadership must honor the person and the ministry by not hiring this individual. They would do the ministry and the individual a great disservice if they hired him or her. The person would either last only a short period of time or stay around and resist the values, increasing the values-erosion process.

Several of the practices that apply to values implementation covered in chapter 6—modeling, visiting, enculturating, training, promoting, rewarding, storytelling, and evaluating—apply to values preservation as well. Review these as you attempt to preserve your ministry's values.

Preserving Values through Prevention
Recruiting
Enfolding

CORRECTION

Correction is needed when values erosion has occurred or is in process. When preventive medicine fails to prevent disease, the doctor shifts to corrective medicine. Now that the patient is ill, what must we do to correct the situation? Does this disruptive situation call for a change of diet, exercise, medication, surgery, chemotherapy, a combination of these, or some other form of treatment?

In spite of all the efforts at preventing values erosion, it too will take place. However, just as doctors and dentists practice corrective medicine, leaders of ministries can practice corrective values preservation. When a leader senses that the values are in the process of eroding or when he or she comes into a ministry situation where the values have already eroded considerably, the leader may respond in the following four ways: challenging, enforcing, defending, and realigning.

Challenging. In spite of an organization's best efforts, sometimes people come into the ministry with a different set of key values. They may have misunderstood the credo, they may have thought they agreed, they may not disagree but do not feel a strong commitment to the values, or they may have lied for some reason. Regardless, the ministry organization must practice corrective medicine; otherwise, doubts about the values' importance will set in and further deterioration is likely.

In this situation, the ministry leaders must challenge people who do not share the organizational values or have not committed to them. Such a challenge will often awake people to the importance of the values and the need for ownership. If nothing else, the credo challenge will heighten their awareness of the values and the need to commit or to move to another ministry where they can find common cause.

In *What Works for Me,* Thomas Horton describes how challenging followers works in the marketplace. In 1979 James Burke, chairman of

Johnson and Johnson, discovered that some on the management team did not embrace the company's core values as found in the credo. This was due primarily to the business's growth and need to hire many new employees. Some had slipped through the cracks. In the following excerpt, Horton presents Burke's credo-challenge process, which works in the ministry world as well as in the marketplace:

> So we began by bringing in about 25 of our managers and laying out to them what we called "The Credo Challenge." What we said, in effect, was this: If you do not really believe in the Credo, and you aren't urging your employees to abide by it, then it is an act of pretension. In that case, you should take it off the walls of your office and throw it away. Then we began the debate, or the challenge as we called it.
>
> We went through every section of the Credo, challenging each one. The assignment was to come out of the meeting either recommending that we get rid of it, change it, or commit to it as it is. And if we were going to change it, I said, "I want you to tell us how." By way of background, you should know that a number of people in the company questioned the wisdom of the challenge meetings. And my predecessor, Dick Sellers, was furious when he found out what we were doing. Only because he didn't feel the Credo should be challenged—he was a real believer in it as it stood. But the meetings became a turn-on, and for two days the debate continued. In the end, the overwhelming majority voted to retain the Credo philosophy but urged some word changes that brought the document more in keeping with the times. In substance, however, the Credo received affirmation. It proved my point that everyone has a value system. But by giving them the opportunity, through discussion and confrontation, to "buy into" the Credo, it was now their philosophy as well, and not one foisted upon them by a previous generation.
>
> The dynamics of that meeting became so important to us, in terms of management involvement in this critical philosophical issue, that over the next three years Dave Clare and I met with all of the other managing directors. The same process ensued, and the results were the same as the first meeting. We then incorporated the recommended word changes into a revised Credo, and reissued it in 1979 at one of our world meetings. We continue the process by holding periodic Credo challenge meetings with new members of senior management soon after they join the company. Dave and I attend these meetings and issue the challenge. There can be no doubt in their minds as to the importance of this business philosophy to the corporation.[2]

Enforcing. Every ministry organization is forced to juggle a number of balls in the air. Two are trust and standards. To a certain degree, leaders must trust their people to know and do the right things. You cannot stand over them all the time making sure they dot every *i* and cross every *t*. People need freedom to act and minister on their own.

The other ball is the ministry's standards. A number of ministries have performance standards for their people; few have values standards. Values standards are more demanding than performance standards because they are the foundation and catalyst for ministry performance. Leaders must address violations of the organizational credo as soon as they occur. The problem often may lie with a miscommunication or misunderstanding of the values. However, if an employee or member is clear on the core beliefs and chooses to violate them, then the leadership must enforce those values. This could involve church or parachurch discipline (Matt. 18:15–35). Evidently the person involved does not share common cause with the ministry. You should help the individual find a ministry that holds the same, or similar, values he or she does.

Every organization must enforce its core values. These values make up the values standards, and they are vital to the life of the ministry. If the leadership fails to separate those who do not hold common values, the values are compromised. In addition, the others who make up the organization will not take them seriously, just as the leadership, by example, has not taken the values seriously.

Defending. Not everyone in a ministry sees the importance of organizational values to that ministry. The concept is a new one for many involved in Christian ministry in the twenty-first century. Therefore, leaders must be ready to defend the concept as well as their credo with their followers.

Perhaps the greatest opposition will come from people who refuse to do anything unless you can show them some precedent in the Scriptures. Although we must look to the Scriptures, often ministries miss numerous opportunities to adopt new paradigms that minister to people in the contemporary culture because Scripture simply does not provide a precedent for everything that takes place in a church or in a parachurch ministry. Much that is taking place in the church is based on its culture and not directly on Scripture. An example is the Sunday service, where a person, called a pastor, stands up and preaches a sermon. This is not to say that this practice is wrong or unbiblical, because it is not. There is nothing wrong with it. However, this approach is very difficult to justify from the Bible.

This is not the problem with the core-values concept, for it is found all over the New Testament, especially in the book of Acts. For example, the church at Jerusalem had a credo, as found in Acts 2:42–47. It also decided a number of issues based on its values. Notable examples are in Acts 6:1–7 and 15:1–35.

Some people will reject the concept because they do not see its importance to their ministries. The same is true of the concept of mission and vision. People are simply not cognizant that their organizational beliefs drive their ministries toward the fulfillment of the vision. They are unaware that core values are behind every decision they make, every problem they resolve, every risk they take. Most have become so busy with their ministries and their demanding schedules that they have little time to stop and think. This is most unfortunate because every leader must have time to think and dream. Chapter 1 is written for them.

Realigning. Often values are affected by misalignments. A values misalignment is an embedded practice, policy, or person (anything or anyone) that is blocking the realization of the ministry values. These misalignments are most detrimental and must be corrected if the ministry is to preserve its central values. How does it work? First, you must identify the values misalignments. I suggest that you form your lay ministry team into groups of two to four people. Then ask the groups to identify the misalignments. Appoint a recorder in each group to list what each group discovers. When the groups are finished, the recorder writes the group's misalignments on a piece of butcher block paper and tapes the paper up on the wall. Then the entire team can identify the misalignments by noting what reoccurs on each sheet of paper. The best approach to realignment is to have the lay ministry team strategize ways to eliminate the misalignments. Thus no person can accuse the pastor of running him or her off or say that the leader opposed his practice or policy.[3]

Preserving Values through Correction

Challenging

Enforcing

Defending

Realigning

Questions for Reflection and Discussion

1. Have you experienced much conflict in your ministry? If yes, how much? Has most of it been interpersonal conflict? Did the early church in Acts experience conflict? Where?
2. In what two ways can a ministry respond to conflict? How has your church responded to conflict? Does your ministry board view its primary job as keeping the peace when there is conflict? If yes, what have been the results?

3. What is wrong with compromise in conflict? What is the result of compromise? What is the difference between compromise and consensus? How do compromise and concession affect an organization's vital values? Have you experienced this in your ministry? If yes, give an example.

4. Which affects you most, opposition from without or from within your ministry? Why? Have you ever encountered any vision vultures or vampires in past ministries? Describe them. Do you have any vision vultures or vampires in your present organization? What effect are they having on the ministry and its values? Are you now or have you ever been a values vulture or vampire?

5. How important is values modeling in your church? Do the leaders model the bottom-line beliefs? Do the leaders live their values when the force of daily realities pressures them? Does your ministry have any values casters? Who are they? Does it use a variety of means to communicate the precepts? Identify some.

6. What is the difference between general and specific values preservation? What is the difference between preventive and corrective values preservation?

7. Do your ministry's core values attract people? If yes, which values? How do you know? Does your church have an enfolding process? What is it? What should you do if an individual does not agree with your values? Define enculturating. How might you enculturate someone in your organization?

8. What is a credo challenge? Could this work for you? Will you try it? Why or why not? Does your church enforce its core beliefs? If yes, how? Have you had to defend the credo or the concept with anyone in the organization? How did it go?

9. Do you need to discover any values misalignments and realign them? If so, will you?

APPENDIX A

CHURCH CREDOS

The Jerusalem Church
Jerusalem, Israel
Bear Valley Church
Denver, Colorado
Carroll Community Church
Westminster, Maryland
Fellowship Bible Church of Dallas
Dallas, Texas
Findlay Evangelical Free Church
Findlay, Ohio
Grace Community Bible Church
Richmond, Texas
Grand Blanc Community Church
Grand Blanc (Detroit), Michigan
Lakeview Community Church
Cedar Hill, Texas
Northwood Community Church
Dallas, Texas
Parkview Evangelical Free Church
Iowa City, Iowa
Saddleback Valley Community Church
Mission Viejo, California
Willow Creek Community Church
South Barrington, Illinois

The Jerusalem Church
Jerusalem, Israel

Core Values

1. **We value** expository teaching (Acts 2:42–43).
2. **We value** fellowship (Acts 2:42).
3. **We value** prayer (Acts 2:42).
4. **We value** biblical community (Acts 2:44–46).
5. **We value** praise and worship (Acts 2:47).
6. **We value** evangelism (Acts 2:47).

Bear Valley Church
Denver, Colorado

Bear Valley's Philosophy of Ministry

1. **Refuge for the Hurting**
   A place where rest and healing is available to those who need it
2. **"Give Us a Place to Stand . . ."**
   A strong home base where personal and family spiritual growth is promoted
3. **Christ-Centered**
   A place that ministers Christ's love and has prayer as the priority
4. **Spirit Determines Structure**
   A place where meeting needs is more important than maintaining programs
5. **Multiple Leadership**
   A place with a team of pastors sharing the leadership
6. **An Unleashed Laity**
   A place where laypeople target specific needs in our city
7. **And We Will Move the World**
   A place that unites target group ministry to the local body
8. **Major Ministries/Modest Facilities**
   A place where modest physical facilities allow time and money to be used for major people ministries
9. **Multiple Congregations**
   A place where small group interaction and nurture are stressed

Carroll Community Church
Westminster, Maryland

1. **Love Jesus Christ**
   No one can love God for us. We must individually stay connected to Christ through an abiding relationship (John 15). Through the Word of God, prayer, personal worship, and obedience we can love God with heart, soul, mind, and strength.

2. **Be Connected through a Small Group**
   Community groups help us develop caring relationships with one another. In this small-group context we can get to know people, hold each other accountable, and offer newcomers a place to belong.

3. **Build Friendships with Non-Christians**
   We can always be on the lookout for ways to reach out with the love of Christ to those who are teetering on the edge of a Christless eternity. By building relationships with non-Christians we may eventually be able to communicate the life-changing message of salvation through Jesus Christ.

4. **Participate on Sunday Mornings**
   Weekly we gather to celebrate God's goodness, be exposed to the Word of God, and catch up on family news. Our contemporary worship services provide ministry to believers and an open door to visitors and non-Christians in the community.

5. **Pray Regularly**
   When we pray we participate in the unseen spiritual world. Ministry is a battleground that needs to be constantly reinforced through prayer.

6. **Give Generously**
   Ministry takes money. Giving may be one of the most tangible expressions of our faith. Believers are encouraged to give generously and sacrificially to the ministry of Carroll Community Church.

7. **Serve Faithfully**
   Christianity is not a spectator sport. Service is love in action. Through our God-given gifts and talents we find fulfillment and participate in the work of God in the world.

Fellowship Bible Church of Dallas
Dallas, Texas

Our Philosophy of Ministry

1. **A Philosophy of Grace**
   You cannot earn God's acceptance. He accepts you now and forever through faith in Jesus Christ. The church should not focus on guilt to motivate its members, but encourage them to live good lives from a motivation of love and thankfulness toward the Lord.
2. **A Christian Self-Image**
   You can have a positive self-image, not because of who you are in yourself, but because of what God has done for you in Jesus Christ.
3. **Biblical Authority**
   You have an authoritative spiritual guide in the Bible, the Word of God. What the Bible teaches takes precedence over church traditions or human opinion.
4. **Communicating Christ to the Contemporary Culture**
   You should be able to understand Christ and the Christian message because it should be communicated to you in a contemporary manner you can identify with and understand. The worship music in the church should be a type of music the contemporary person can relate to and understand.
5. **Balanced Christianity**
   You need a balanced Christian experience which includes meaningful worship, life-related biblical teaching, significant relationships with other Christians, and serving others according to your gifts, abilities, and interests.
6. **Every Christian Is a Minister**
   You, along with every other Christian, possess natural talents and spiritual gifts. As you release these talents and gifts for God to use, you will find more significance and purpose in your life.
7. **Every Christian Should Be a World Christian**
   You should be concerned to spread the Christian message to people of other cultures than your own, so they can share the same Christ who has helped you.

Findlay Evangelical Free Church
Findlay, Ohio

Distinctives of Findlay Evangelical Free Church

1. **A commitment to** creative forms and nontraditional methods of ministry
2. **A commitment to** godly leadership
3. **A commitment to** encouraging all believers to utilize their spiritual gifts
4. **A commitment to** a Bible-centered teaching ministry
5. **A commitment to** cultivating a Christ-like and loving atmosphere within the body
6. **A commitment to** helping Christians develop a life of godliness in all areas of Christian living
7. **A commitment to** meeting the material needs of those in serious need, both within and outside our own body
8. **A commitment to** cultivating deep, abiding relationships within the body of Christ
9. **A commitment to** unity, love, and forgiveness among believers

Grace Community Bible Church
Richmond, Texas

Our Core Values

1. **A Dedication to Purpose**
   Our purpose is to lead people to salvation in Christ and growth in Christ-likeness.
2. **A Dedication to People**
   God works through people, and each person is unique and vital to God's plan.
3. **A Dedication to Relationships**
   Building relationships is indispensable to spiritual birth and spiritual growth.
4. **A Dedication to Innovation**
   While our message is timeless, our methods adapt to those we are here to serve.
5. **A Dedication to Quality**
   In everything we do, we give God only our best.

Grand Blanc Community Church
Grand Blanc (Detroit), Michigan

To help keep us on track with our mission:

1. **We deeply value** the people of Grand Blanc.
2. **We deeply value** the truth and applicability of the Bible, God's Word to humankind.
3. **We deeply value** cultural relevance and involvement.
4. **We deeply value** personal authenticity and integrity.
5. **We deeply value** excellence at every level.
6. **We deeply value** the importance of healthy relationships, both with God and with one another.

Lakeview Community Church
Cedar Hill, Texas

This statement of principles clarifies the attitudes and approaches that will be encouraged in the ministries of Lakeview Community Church. Most of these are not biblical absolutes, but they represent our understanding of how to most effectively accomplish our purpose.

1. **A Commitment to Relevant Bible Exposition**
   We believe that the Bible is God's inspired Word, the authoritative and trustworthy rule of faith and practice for Christians. The Bible is both timeless and timely, relevant to the common needs of all people at all times and to the specific problems of contemporary living. Therefore, we are committed to equipping Christians, through the preaching and teaching of God's Word, to follow Christ in every sphere of life.
2. **A Commitment to Prayer**
   We believe that God desires his people to pray and that he hears and answers prayer (Matt. 7:7–11; James 5:13–18). Therefore, the ministries and activities of this church will be characterized by a reliance on prayer in their conception, planning, and execution.
3. **A Commitment to Lay Ministry**
   We believe that the primary responsibility of the pastor(s) and teachers in the local church is to "prepare God's people for works of service" (Eph. 4:12). Therefore, the ministry of Lakeview Community Church will be placed as much as possible in the hands of nonvocational workers. This will be accomplished through training opportunities and through practices which encourage lay

initiation, leadership, responsibility, and authority in the various ministries of the church.

4. **A Commitment to Small Groups**
   We are committed to small-group ministry as one of the most effective means of building relationships, stimulating spiritual growth, and developing leaders.

5. **An Appreciation for Creativity and Innovation**
   In today's rapidly changing world, forms and methods must be continually evaluated, and if necessary, altered to fit new conditions. While proven techniques should not be discarded at a whim, we encourage creativity and innovation, flexibility and adaptability. We are more concerned with effectiveness in ministry than with adherence to tradition.

6. **A Commitment to Excellence**
   We believe that the God of our salvation deserves the best we have to offer. The Lord himself is a God of excellence, as shown by the beauty of creation; further, he gave the best that he had, his only son, for us (Rom. 8:32). Paul exhorts servants, in whatever they do, to "work at it with all your heart, as working for the Lord, not for men" (Col. 3:23). Therefore, in the ministries and activities of Lakeview Community Church we will seek to maintain a high standard of excellence to the glory of God. This will be achieved when every person is exercising his or her God-given spiritual gift to the best of his or her ability (1 Cor. 12).

7. **A Commitment to Growth**
   Although numerical growth is not necessarily a sign of God's blessing, and is not a sufficient goal in itself, we believe that God desires for us to reach as many people as possible with the life-changing message of Jesus Christ. Therefore, we will pursue methods and policies which will facilitate numerical growth, without compromising in any way our integrity or our commitment to biblical truth.

Northwood Community Church
Dallas, Texas

The following presents both the actual and aspirational values of Northwood Community Church. The following define and drive our ministry in the context of a warm and caring environment.

We Value Christ's Headship
We acknowledge Christ as head of our church and submit ourselves and all our activities to His will and good pleasure (Eph. 1:22–23).

We Value Biblical Teaching

We strive to teach God's Word with integrity and authority so that seekers find Christ and believers mature in Him (2 Tim. 3:16).

We Value Authentic Worship

We desire to acknowledge God's supreme value and worth in our personal lives and in the corporate, contemporary worship of our church (Rom. 12:1–2).

We Value Prayer

We rely on private and corporate prayer in the conception, planning, and execution of all the ministries and activities of this church (Matt. 7:7–11).

We Value Community

We ask all our people to commit to and fully participate in biblically functioning small groups where they may reach the lost, exercise their gifts, be shepherded, and thus grow in Christ-likeness (Acts 2:44–46).

We Value Family

We support the spiritual nurture of the family as one of God's dynamic means to perpetuate the Christian faith (2 Tim. 1:5).

As a church community, we at Northwood aspire to the following values:

We Value a Mobilized Congregation

We seek to equip all our uniquely designed and gifted people to effectively accomplish the work of our ministry (Eph. 4:11–13).

We Value Lost People

We value unchurched, lost people and will use every available Christ honoring means to pursue, win, and grow them to maturity in the faith (Luke 19:10).

Parkview Evangelical Free Church
Iowa City, Iowa

Parkview's Values

1. **Scripture**
   A *biblical message:* We are committed to the clear and accurate communication of God's Word in a way that ministers grace and urges obedience (2 Tim. 3:16–17).
2. **Creativity**
   A *fresh approach:* We are committed to forms of worship and ministry that will best capture and express what God is doing in our generation and culture (Luke 5:33–39).
3. **Ministry**
   A *team effort:* We are committed to a team model for ministry and organization that equips and empowers every family, member, and leader (Eph. 4:11–16).

Saddleback Valley Community Church
Mission Viejo, California

Our Statement of Values

We Are a Purpose-Driven, Value-Based Church

1. **We Value the Application of Scripture**
   "Do not merely listen to the word, and so deceive yourselves. Do what it says" (James 1:22).
2. **We Value Service**
   "Your attitude must be like my own, for I, the Messiah, did not come to be served, but to serve" (Matt. 20:28 TLB).
   "David had served God's purpose in his own generation" (Acts 13:36).
   "Let love make you serve one another" (Gal. 5:13 GNT).
3. **We Value Excellence**
   "Each one should test his own actions. Then he can take pride in himself, without comparing himself to somebody else" (Gal. 6:4).
   "The quality of each person's work will be seen when the Day of Christ exposes it" (1 Cor. 3:13 GNT).

4. **We Value Feedback**
   "A fool thinks he needs no advice, but a wise man listens to others" (Prov. 12:15 TLB).
   "Get the facts at any price" (Prov. 23:23 TLB).
   "Every prudent man acts out of knowledge" (Prov. 13:16).
   "Be sure you know the condition of your flocks, give careful attention to your herds" (Prov. 27:23).
   "Reliable communication permits progress" (Prov. 13:17 TLB).
5. **We Value Authenticity**
   "Our lives in this world, and especially our relations with you, have been ruled by God-given frankness and sincerity" (2 Cor. 1:12 GNT).
   "We are hiding nothing from you and our hearts are absolutely open to you" (2 Cor. 6:11 PHILLIPS).
6. **We Value Informality**
   "A relaxed attitude lengthens a man's life" (Prov. 14:30 TLB).
7. **We Value People's Giftedness**
   "God has given each of us the ability to do certain things well" (Rom. 12:6 TLB).
   "Each one should use whatever gift he has received to serve others" (1 Peter 4:10).
8. **We Value People's Differences**
   "There are all sorts of service to be done, but always to the same Lord; working in all sorts of different ways in different people" (1 Cor. 12:5 JB).
   "Accept one another, then, just as Christ accepted you" (Rom. 15:7).
   "Live together in harmony, live together in love, as though you have only one mind and one spirit between you" (Phil. 2:2).
9. **We Value Continual Learning**
   "He who loves wisdom loves his own best interest and will be a success" (Prov. 19:8 TLB).
   "If the ax is dull, and its edge unsharpened, more strength is needed but skill will bring success" (Eccles. 10:10).
10. **We Value Simplicity**
    "God made us plain and simple, but we have made ourselves very complicated" (Eccles. 7:29 GNT).
    "When I came to you, it was not with any show of oratory or philosophy, but *simply* to tell you what God has guaranteed" (1 Cor. 2:1 JB).
11. **We Value Teamwork**
    "Now you are the body of Christ, and each one of you is a part of it" (1 Cor. 12:27).

"Two are better off than one, because together they can work more effectively" (Eccles. 4:9 GNT).

"In Christ we who are many form one body, and each member belongs to all the others" (Rom. 12:5).

12. **We Value Innovation**
"The intelligent man is always open to new ideas. In fact, he looks for them" (Prov. 18:15 TLB).

13. **We Value Freedom and Flexibility**
"Where the Spirit of the Lord is, there is freedom" (2 Cor. 3:17).
"We may make our plans, but God has the last word" (Prov. 16:1 GNT).

14. **We Value Humor**
"Being cheerful keeps you healthy. It is slow death to be gloomy all the time" (Prov. 17:22 GNT).
"God . . . richly provides us with everything for our enjoyment" (1 Tim. 6:17).

15. **We Value Optimism**
"All things are possible with God" (Mark 10:27).
"According to your faith will it be done to you" (Matt. 9:29).

16. **We Value Growth**
"Under Christ's control, the whole body is nourished and held together . . . and it grows as God wants it to grow" (Col. 2:19 GNT).

17. **We Value Commitment**
"First they gave themselves to the Lord; and then, by God's will they gave themselves to us as well" (2 Cor. 8:5 GNT).

Willow Creek Community Church
South Barrington, Illinois

1. **We believe** that anointed teaching is the catalyst for transformation in individuals' lives and in the church.
2. **We believe** that lost people matter to God, and, therefore, ought to matter to the church.
3. **We believe** that the church should be culturally relevant while remaining doctrinally pure.
4. **We believe** that Christ's followers should manifest authenticity and yearn for continuous growth.
5. **We believe** that a church should operate as a unified community of servants stewarding their spiritual gifts.
6. **We believe** that loving relationships should permeate every aspect of church life.
7. **We believe** that life-change happens best in small groups.

8. **We believe** that excellence honors God and inspires people.
9. **We believe** that churches should be led by those with leadership gifts.
10. **We believe** that full devotion to Christ and His cause is normal for every believer.

PARACHURCH CREDOS

CAM International
Dallas, Texas
Denver Seminary
Denver, Colorado
Sonlife Ministries
Wheaton, Illinois

CAM International
Dallas, Texas

Corporate Values

1. **Biblical and Theological Foundations**
   We view every ministry and relationship through the lens of Holy Scripture to insure that our Mission remains biblically based and theologically sound. Our doctrinal foundation guides our practice.

2. **Prayer**

   We believe that prayer is our most fundamental demonstration of worship and dependence on the Lord. As a faith Mission, we sustain every ministry in continuous personal and corporate prayer centered in thanksgiving, praise, and intercession.

3. **Integrity**

   We strive to develop Christian character and a Christ-like manner in all that we do, living and working above reproach.

4. **Vision**

   We will take the initiative to seek opportunities to extend CAM's personnel and expertise into new fields and new areas of ministry where our service can be of strategic value.

5. **Innovation**

   We believe in a pioneering spirit characterized by creative methods, openness to risk, aggressive expansion, proactive attitudes, and application of biblical truth to changing needs.

6. **Excellence**

   We strive toward excellence, reflected in the quality of our personnel and in the efficient use of the most appropriate technology in ministry.

7. **People**

   We value people. We recognize the eternal value of every individual. We commit ourselves to love and care for each other with sensitivity and humility within our Mission and among the national brethren with whom we serve.

8. **Family**

   We are committed to supporting the development and nurture of the family.

9. **Teamwork**

   We are committed to teamwork in all relationships based on a common vision that permits diversity and flexibility in unity and fosters internationalization and full synergy of gifts and talents.

10. **Evangelism**

    We are committed to bring the gospel to the lost by all available means.

11. **Discipleship**

    We seek to fulfill Christ's command to "make disciples." It is our purpose to build up the body of Christ by living example and effective training.

12. **Church**

    We believe the local church is the unique and divinely ordained instrument on earth in God's purpose to glorify Himself. We respect, edify, and cooperate with like-minded churches at home and abroad.

13. **Partnership**

We are committed to partnership with like-minded mission agencies and national sending churches. We freely share information, personnel, and resources and pursue effective joint ministry projects in an outreach to the whole world.

14. **Unity**

We are committed to unity within CAM and with other like-minded believers. "Being diligent to preserve the unity of the Spirit in the bond of peace," we work together without compromise to fulfill God's perfect will.

15. **Servanthood**

We are, above all, servants of our Lord Jesus Christ. We give ourselves to the highest good for our brothers in Christ and the community in which we live. We are committed to a Christ-like love expressed in all we are and do.

Denver Seminary
Denver, Colorado

Values

1. **We are committed to**
   training people for diverse ministries in and alongside of local churches.

2. **We are committed to**
   upholding teaching as the professors' primary task.

3. **We are committed to**
   promoting the maximum utilization of faculty gifts of leadership and scholarship to serve God's redemptive purposes.

4. **We are committed to**
   providing graduate level education in which scholarship is placed in the service of ministry.

5. **We are committed to**
   applying in the classroom adult education principles which wed relevant theory to the practice of ministry.

6. **We are committed to**
   employing biblical truth in critiquing and addressing cultures.

7. **We are committed to**
   fostering the moral and spiritual formation of students.

Sonlife Ministries
Wheaton, Illinois

Our Values

1. Christ commanded me to make disciples—it isn't an option.
2. Christ—through His life—modeled for me the process of fulfilling the Great Commission. Making disciples involves seeking the lost, establishing believers, and equipping workers: An ongoing balance of winning, building, and equipping priorities, programs and relationships.
3. Dependence upon God—through His Word, prayer, and His Holy Spirit—is essential to fulfill my part in His Great Commission.
4. The Great Commission is my individual responsibility. In its most critical and basic form, the Great Commission is peer-to-peer, friend-to-friend and expands from me to the ends of the earth.
5. My love for God and for others motivates me to Great-Commission living.
6. The church is God's chosen vehicle to assist and equip me in the fulfillment of this God-given responsibility.

MARKETPLACE CREDOS

Herman Miller, Inc.
Hewlett-Packard
The Johnson and Johnson Company
Merck and Company

Herman Miller, Inc.

Core Values and Beliefs

We are a research-driven product company; we are not a market-driven company.

We intend to make a contribution to society, through our products, services, and the way we deliver them.

We are dedicated to quality: quality of product, quality of service, quality of relationships, quality of our communications, quality of our promises.

We believe that we should be, for all who are involved, a place of realized potential.

We cannot live our lives isolated from the needs of society.

We are deeply committed to the Scanlon idea, a plan for practicing participative management, including productivity and profit sharing.

Profit, like breathing, is indispensable. While it is not the sole goal
of our lives, in the context of our opportunities, profit must be a
result of our contribution.

Hewlett-Packard

Core Values and Beliefs

In the words of Dave Packard:
"The HP Way says, 'Do unto others as you would have them do unto
you.' That's really what it's all about."

In the words of Bill Hewlett:
"Fundamentally, the HP Way is respect for the individual. If you
give him a chance, the individual will do a lot more than you think he
can. So you give him the freedom. Respect for the individual—not just
employees, but customers and the works."

The Johnson and Johnson Company

Credo

We believe that our first responsibility is to our customers.

Our second responsibility is to our employees.

Our third responsibility is to our management.

Our fourth responsibility is to the communities in which we live. We
must be a good citizen.

Our fifth and last responsibility is to our stockholders.

Business must make a sound profit. When we operate according to
our principles, stockholders should realize a fair return.

We are determined with the help of God's grace to fulfill these obliga-
tions to the best of our ability.

Merck and Company

Core Values

We value above all our integrity to serve the patient.

We are committed to the highest standards of ethics and integrity.

We are responsible to our customers, to our employees, and to the societies we serve.

Our interactions with all segments of society—customers, suppliers, governments, and the general public—must reflect the high standards we profess.

We are committed to research that matches science to the needs of humanity.

Since our future as a company rests squarely on the knowledge, imagination, skills, teamwork, and integrity of our employees, we value these qualities most highly.

We expect profit, but profit from work that benefits humanity.

APPENDIX D

CORE VALUES AUDITS

Personal Ministry Core Values Audit

Using the scale below, circle the number that best expresses to what extent the following values are important to you (actual values)—you would want them to be a part of the church you attend. Work your way through the list quickly, going with your first impression.

1	2	3	4
not important	somewhat important	important	most important

1. **Fairness:** Being treated impartially, without bias or prejudice   1 2 3 4
2. **Family:** People immediately related to one another by marriage or birth   1 2 3 4
3. **Bible knowledge:** A familiarity with the truths of the Scriptures   1 2 3 4
4. **World missions:** Spreading the gospel of Christ around the globe   1 2 3 4
5. **Community:** Caring about and addressing the needs of others   1 2 3 4
6. **Encouragement:** Giving hope to people who need some hope   1 2 3 4
7. **Giving:** Providing a portion of one's finances to support the ministry   1 2 3 4
8. **Relationships:** People getting along with one another   1 2 3 4

9. **Leadership:** A person's ability to influence others to pursue God's mission for their organization   1 2 3 4

10. **Cultural relevance:** Communicating truth in a way that people who aren't like us understand it   1 2 3 4

11. **Prayer:** Communicating with God   1 2 3 4

12. **Excellence:** Maintaining the highest of ministry standards that brings glory to God   1 2 3 4

13. **Evangelism:** Telling others the good news about Christ   1 2 3 4

14. **Team ministry:** A group of people ministering together   1 2 3 4

15. **Creativity:** Coming up with new ideas and ways of doing ministry   1 2 3 4

16. **Worship:** Attributing worth to God   1 2 3 4

17. **Status quo:** A preference for the way things are now   1 2 3 4

18. **Cooperation:** The act of working together in the service of the Savior   1 2 3 4

19. **Lost people:** People who are nonChristians and may not attend church (unchurched)   1 2 3 4

20. **Mobilized laity:** Christians who are actively serving in the ministries of their church   1 2 3 4

21. **Tradition:** The customary ways or the "tried and true"   1 2 3 4

22. **Obedience:** A willingness to do what God or others ask of a person   1 2 3 4

23. **Innovation:** Making changes that promote the ministry as it serves Christ   1 2 3 4

24. **Initiative:** The willingness to take the first step or make the first move in a ministry situation   1 2 3 4

25. **Other values:**

Write below all the values that you rated with a 3 or 4. Rank these according to priority. The first six are your core values.

Church Ministry Core Values Audit

Using the scale below, circle the number that best expresses to what extent the following values are important to your church (actual values)—they characterize the church you attend. Work your way through the list quickly, going with your first impression.

1	2	3	4
not important	somewhat important	important	most important

1. **Fairness:** Being treated impartially, without bias or prejudice   1 2 3 4

2. **Family:** People immediately related to one another by marriage or birth 1 2 3 4

3. **Bible knowledge:** A familiarity with the truths of the Scriptures   1 2 3 4

4. **World missions:** Spreading the gospel of Christ around the globe   1 2 3 4

5. **Community:** Caring about and addressing the needs of others	1 2 3 4
6. **Encouragement:** Giving hope to people who need some hope	1 2 3 4
7. **Giving:** Providing a portion of one's finances to support the ministry	1 2 3 4
8. **Relationships:** People getting along with one another	1 2 3 4
9. **Leadership:** A person's ability to influence others to pursue God's mission for their organization	1 2 3 4
10. **Cultural relevance:** Communicating truth in a way that people who aren't like us understand it	1 2 3 4
11. **Prayer:** Communicating with God	1 2 3 4
12. **Excellence:** Maintaining the highest of ministry standards that brings glory to God	1 2 3 4
13. **Evangelism:** Telling others the good news about Christ	1 2 3 4
14. **Team ministry:** A group of people ministering together	1 2 3 4
15. **Creativity:** Coming up with new ideas and ways of doing ministry	1 2 3 4
16. **Worship:** Attributing worth to God	1 2 3 4
17. **Status quo:** A preference for the way things are now	1 2 3 4
18. **Cooperation:** The act of working together in the service of the Savior	1 2 3 4
19. **Lost people:** People who are non-Christians and may not attend church (unchurched)	1 2 3 4
20. **Mobilized laity:** Christians who are actively serving in the ministries of their church	1 2 3 4
21. **Tradition:** The customary ways or the "tried and true"	1 2 3 4
22. **Obedience:** A willingness to do what God or others ask of a person	1 2 3 4
23. **Innovation:** Making changes that promote the ministry as it serves Christ	1 2 3 4
24. **Initiative:** The willingness to take the first step or make the first move in a ministry situation	1 2 3 4

25. **Other values:**

Write below all the values that you rated with a 3 or 4. Rank these according to priority. The first six are your church's core values.

READINESS FOR CHANGE INVENTORY

E ven the most dynamic church can become resistant to necessary, healthy change. However, churches must change if they are to have significant impact on their communities. Is your church ready for change?

Each item below is a key element that will help you evaluate your church's readiness for change. Strive for objectivity—involve others (including outsiders) in the evaluation process. Circle the number that most accurately rates your church.

1. **Leadership.** The pastor and the church board (official leadership) are favorable toward and directly responsible for change. Also, if any influential persons (unofficial leadership: the church patriarch, a wealthy member, for example) are for change, score 5. If moderately so, score 3. If only the secondary level of leadership (other staff, Sunday school teachers, etc.) is for change while unofficial leadership opposes it, score 1.

   5 3 1

2. **Vision.** The pastor and the board have a single, clear vision of a significant future that looks different from the present. If the pastor is able to mobilize most relevant parties (other staff, boards, and the congregation) for action, score 5. If the pastor but not

the board envisions a different direction for the church, score 3.
If the pastor and board have not thought about a vision, and/or
they do not believe that it is important, score 1.

5 3 1

3. **Values.** The church's philosophy of ministry (its core values)
includes a preference for innovation and creativity. Though proven
forms, methods, and techniques are not discarded at a whim, the
church is more concerned with the effectiveness of its ministries
than with adherence to traditions, score 5. If moderately so, score
3. If the church's ministry forms and techniques have changed
little over the years while its ministry effectiveness has dimin-
ished, score 1.

5 3 1

4. **Motivation.** The pastor and the board have a strong sense of
urgency for change that is shared by the congregation. If the congregational culture emphasizes the need for constant improvement,
score 3. If the pastor and/or the board (most of whom have been
in their positions for many years) along with the congregation are
bound by long-standing traditions that are change-resistant and
discourage risk taking, score 1. If somewhere between, score 2.

3 2 1

5. **Organizational Context.** How does the change effort affect
the other programs in the church (Christian education, worship,
missions, and others)? If the individuals in charge are all working
together for improvement and innovation, score 3. If some are,
score 2. If many are opposed to change or are in conflict with one
another over change, score 1.

3 2 1

6. **Processes/Functions.** Major changes in a church almost always
require redesigning processes and functions in all the ministries
of the church, such as Christian education, church worship, and
others. If most in charge of these areas are open to change, score
3. If only some, score 2. If they are turf protectors, or if they put
their areas of ministry ahead of the church as a whole, score 1.

3 2 1

7. **Ministry Awareness.** Does the leadership of your church keep
up with what is taking place in the innovative evangelical churches
in the community and across America in terms of ministry and
outreach effectiveness? Does the leadership objectively compare
what it is doing to that of churches that are very similar to it? If
the answer is yes, score 3. If the answer is sometimes, score 2. If
no, score 1.

3 2 1

8. **Community Focus.** Does the church know and understand the people in the community—their needs, hopes, aspirations? Does it stay in direct contact with them? Does it regularly seek to reach them? If the answer is yes, score 3. If moderately so, score 2. If the church is not in touch with its community and focuses primarily on itself, score 1.

3 2 1

9. **Evaluation.** Does the church regularly evaluate its ministries? Does it evaluate its ministries in light of its vision and goals? Are these ministries regularly adjusted in response to the evaluations? If all of this takes place, score 3. If some takes place, score 2. If none, score 1.

3 2 1

10. **Rewards.** Change is easier if the leaders and those involved in ministry are rewarded in some way for taking risks and looking for new solutions to their ministry problems. Also, rewarding ministry teams is more effective than rewarding solo performances. If this characterizes your church, score 3. If it happens sometimes, score 2. If your church rewards the status quo and a maintenance mentality, score 1.

3 2 1

11. **Organizational Structure.** The best situation is a flexible church where change is well received and takes place periodically, not every day. If this is true of your church, score 3. If your church is very rigid in its structure and either has changed very little in the last five years or has experienced several futile attempts at change to no avail, score 1. If between, score 2.

3 2 1

12. **Communication.** Does your church have a variety of means for two-way communication? Do most understand and use it, and does it reach all levels of the congregation? If this is true, score 3. If only moderately true, score 2. If communication is poor, primarily one-way and from the top down, score 1.

3 2 1

13. **Organizational Hierarchy.** Is your church decentralized (has few if any levels of leadership between the congregation and the pastor or the board)? If so, score 3. If there are people on staff levels or boards/committees who come between the congregation and the pastor or the board, more potential exists for them to block essential change, score 1. If between, score 2.

3 2 1

14. **Prior Change.** Churches will most readily adapt to change if they have successfully implemented major changes in the recent past.

If this is true of your church, score 3. If some change, score 2. If
no one can remember the last time the church changed, or if such
efforts failed or left people angry and resentful, score 1.

3 2 1

15. **Morale.** Do the church staff and volunteers enjoy the church and
take responsibility for their ministries? Do they trust the pastor
and the board? If so, score 3. If moderately so, score 2. Do few
people volunteer and are there signs of low team spirit? Is there
mistrust between leaders and followers and between the various
ministries? If so, score 1.

3 2 1

16. **Innovation.** The church tries new things. People feel free to implement new ideas on a consistent basis. People have the freedom
to make choices and solve problems regarding their ministries.
If this describes your church, score 3. If this is somewhat true,
score 2. If ministries are ensnared in bureaucratic red tape and
permission from on high must be obtained before anything happens, score 1.

3 2 1

17. **Decision Making.** Does the church leadership listen carefully
to a wide variety of suggestions from all the congregation? After
it has gathered the appropriate information, does it make decisions quickly? If so, score 3. If moderately so, score 2. Does
the leadership listen only to a select few and take forever to
make a decision? Is there a lot of conflict during the process,
and after a decision is made, is there confusion and turmoil?
If so, score 1.

3 2 1

Total Score:_____

If your score is:

47–57: The chances are good that you can implement change, especially if your scores are high on items 1–3.

28–46: Change may take place but with varying success. Chances
increase the higher the scores are on items 1–3. Note areas with low
scores and focus on improvement before attempting change on a large
scale.

17–27: Change will not likely take place. Note areas with low
scores and attempt to improve them if possible. Consider starting a
new church and implementing your ideas in a more change-friendly
context.

For additional copies, write or call:

The Malphurs Group
7916 Briar Brook Ct.
Dallas, TX 75218
214-841-3777
www.malphursgroup.com

Cost: $3.00 per copy (includes postage and handling)

NOTES

Introduction

1. Thomas J. Peters and Robert H. Waterman Jr., *In Search of Excellence* (New York: Warner Books, 1982), 281.

2. Consequently, this book will not contain as many notes as some of my other writings. Harold Westing includes an informative chapter on core values in his book *Create and Celebrate Your Church's Uniqueness* (Grand Rapids: Kregel, 1993).

3. Aubrey Malphurs, *Developing a Vision for Ministry in the 21st Century* (Grand Rapids: Baker, 1992). Although I had not seen a copy, the only other book on vision that I was aware of at the time was Robert Dale's *To Dream Again* (Nashville: Broadman Press, 1981).

Chapter 1 You Can't Live without Them

1. Lyle E. Schaller, *Getting Things Done* (Nashville: Abingdon Press, 1986), 152.

2. See Aubrey Malphurs, *Vision America: A Strategy for Reaching a Nation* (Grand Rapids: Baker, 1994), 74–80, for more information about the change from modernism to postmodernism in America.

3. Schaller, *Getting Things Done*, 153.

4. Jennifer A. Chatman, "Improving Interactional Organizational Research: A Model of Person-Organization Fit," *Academy of Management Review* 14, no. 3 (1969): 333.

5. James M. Kouzes and Barry Z. Posner, *Credibility* (San Francisco: Jossey-Bass, 1993), 66.

6. Amy C. Edmondson, "When Company Values Backfire," *Harvard Business Review* 80, no. 11 (November 2002): 18–19.

7. James C. Collins and William C. Lazier, *Beyond Entrepreneurship: Turning Your Business into an Enduring Great Company* (Englewood Cliffs, NJ: Prentice Hall, 1992), 66.

8. Aubrey Malphurs, *Advanced Strategic Planning: A New Model for Church and Ministry Leaders* (Grand Rapids: Baker, 1999).

Chapter 2 What Are We Talking About?

1. Jay Matthews, "Much Ado about Nothing?" *Washington Post,* January 8, 1995.

2. I observed in the 1980s and 1990s that the tendency among churches was to shorten and broaden what used to be rather precise and lengthy doctrinal statements. Now the statements appear to be more inclusive than exclusive, reflecting the desire of churches to accept more people than to reject them.

3. Milton Rokeach, *The Nature of Human Values* (New York: Free Press, 1973), 5.

4. Researchers such as Charles O'Reilly et al. express general agreement with my working definition. They write, "Basic values may be thought of as internalized normative beliefs that can guide behavior." Charles A. O'Reilly III, Jennifer Chatman, and David F. Caldwell, "People and Organizational Culture: A Profile Comparison Approach to Assessing Person-Organization Fit," *Academy of Management Journal* 34, no. 3 (1991): 492. Patrick Lencioni is also close when he defines a value as "deeply ingrained principles that guide all of a company's actions." Patrick M. Lencioni, "Make Your Values Mean Something," *Harvard Business Review* (July 2002): 114.

5. Frank B. Withrow, "Guest Editorial," *T.H.E. Journal* 21, no. 3 (September 1993): 10.

6. John M. Woodyard, "A 21st Century Seminary Faculty Model" (review of graduate theological education in the Pacific Northwest for the M. J. Murdock Charitable Trust, Vancouver, WA, 1994), 4.

7. O'Reilly III, Chatman, and Caldwell, "People and Organizational Culture," 493.

8. Ibid.

9. Jeanne Liedtka, "Value Congruence: The Interplay of Individual and Organizational Value Systems," *Journal of Business Ethics* 8 (1989): 805–15.

10. Schaller, *Getting Things Done,* 153.

11. Ibid.

12. K. A. Jehn, C. Chadwick, and S. Thatcher, "To Agree or Not to Agree: The Effects of Value Congruence, Individual Demographic, Dissimilarity, and Conflict on Workgroup Outcomes," *International Journal of Conflict Management* 8 (October 1997): 287–305.

13. Bruce Megliano, Elizabeth Ravlin, and Cheryl Adkins, "Value Congruence and Satisfaction with a Leader: An Examination of the Role of Interaction," *Human Relations* 44 (1991): 48.

14. W. Randy Boxx, Randall Odom, and Mark Dunn, "Organizational Values and Value Congruency and Their Impact on Satisfaction, Commitment, and

Cohesion: An Empirical Examination within the Public Sector," *Public Personnel Management* 20 (summer 1991): 195–205.

15. P. Harrison, "Pastoral Turnover and the Call to Preach," *Jets* 44 (March 2001): 87.

16. George Barna, *The Second Coming of the Church* (Nashville: Word, 1998).

17. A. King, "Multiphase Progression of Organizational Ideology and Commitment," *Mid-Atlantic Journal of Business* 31 (June 1995): 143–60.

18. Stephen R. Covey, *The 7 Habits of Highly Effective People* (New York: Simon and Schuster, 1989), 72.

19. Peters and Waterman, *In Search of Excellence,* 280.

20. James M. Kouzes and Barry Z. Posner, *The Leadership Challenge* (San Francisco: Jossey-Bass, 1987), 193.

21. Chatman, "Improving Interactional Organizational Research," 344.

22. Ibid.

23. Westing, *Create and Celebrate Your Church's Uniqueness,* 29.

Chapter 3 What Drives You?

1. Chatman, "Improving Interactional Organizational Research," 341.

2. Some note that it's usually women who teach the primary classes. They believe that it is important to the children that men involve themselves more, providing good role models, especially for the boys in these classes.

3. Rokeach, *Nature of Human Values.*

4. Paul McDonald and Jeffrey Gandz, "Identification of Values Relevant to Business Research," *Human Resource Management* 30 (summer 1991): 226.

5. These ministry circumstances are rare. However, one such circumstance would be where the organization is dying and the people and leadership know it. If something does not happen soon, the ministry is history. Consequently, they are more open to change and are willing to adopt new values.

6. Chatman, "Improving Interactional Organizational Research," 343.

7. Ibid., 342.

8. H. Weiss, "Social Learning of Work Values in Organizations," *Journal of Applied Psychology* 63 (1978): 63.

9. Chatman, "Improving Interactional Organizational Research," 338.

10. M. Kohn and C. Schooler, "The Reciprocal Effects of the Substantive Complexity of Work and Intellectual Flexibility: A Longitudinal Assessment," *American Journal of Sociology* 84 (1978): 84.

11. Chatman, "Improving Interactional Organizational Research," 343.

12. Ibid., 344.

13. Ibid., 343.

Chapter 4 Writing Your Values Credo

1. Dave Francis and Mike Woodcock, *Unblocking Organizational Values* (Glenview, FL: Scott, Foresman, 1990), 33.

2. Collins and Lazier, *Beyond Entrepreneurship,* 66.

3. "Tomorrow's Church . . . the Best of Both Worlds," *Compass* 3 (for the Church of the 21st Century Conference, Minneapolis, MN, February 1994), 1.

4. Thomas J. Watson Jr., *A Business and Its Beliefs: Ideas That Helped Build IBM* (New York: McGraw-Hill, 1963), 39.

5. James C. Collins and Jerry I. Porras, *Built to Last* (New York: Harper Business, 1994), 219.

6. Ibid., 74.

7. Ibid.

Chapter 5 Moving Your Values from Paper to People

1. Many believe that the gifts in Ephesians 4:11 belong to the professional ministry. For example, pastors are thought to be the gifted prophets, traveling professional evangelists are the evangelists, and seminary professors hold the teaching office. I do not see justification for this view anywhere in the text. Certainly laypeople (a term I dislike) have these gifts as well and could exercise them within and outside the body of Christ.

2. J. William Pfeiffer, Leonard D. Goodstein, and Timothy M. Nolan, *Shaping Strategic Planning: Frogs, Dragons, Bees, and Turkey Tails* (San Diego: Scott, Foresman, 1989), 109.

3. Ibid. The authors suggest these roles. I have developed them further in the context of ministry.

4. Malphurs, *Developing a Vision for Ministry,* chapter 5.

5. I discuss leadership styles in *Maximizing Your Effectiveness: How to Discover and Develop Your Divine Design* (Grand Rapids: Baker, 1995), chapter 3.

6. Alan L. Wilkins, *Developing Corporate Character* (San Francisco: Jossey-Bass, 1989), 97.

7. Ibid.

8. Joseph L. Badaracco Jr. and Richard R. Ellsworth, *Leadership and the Quest for Integrity* (Boston: Harvard Business School Press, 1989), 90.

9. Wilkins, *Developing Corporate Character,* 98.

10. Kouzes and Posner, *The Leadership Challenge,* 207.

11. You may purchase this tape and others at a reasonable cost directly from Seeds, Willow Creek's tape ministry. They are well worth the cost. (Willow Creek Community Church Seeds Tape Ministry, 67 East Algonquin Road, South Barrington, IL 60010; 708-382-6208).

12. Kouzes and Posner, *The Leadership Challenge,* 261.

13. Ibid., 262.

Chapter 6 Weaving New Values into the Congregational Fabric

1. C. Wayne Zunkel, *Growing the Small Church* (Elgin, IL: David C. Cook, 1982), 48.

2. Kevin B. Blackstone, "Taking a Demographic Look at Dallas," *Dallas Morning News,* June 29, 1989.

3. George G. Hunter III, *How to Reach Secular People* (Nashville: Abingdon Press, 1992), 28–29.

4. Erwin R. McManus, "Urban Shift," *The Power of Seeing* 1, no. 1.

5. Frank R. Tillapaugh, *Unleashing the Church* (Ventura, CA: Regal, 1982).

6. Joel Arthur Barker, *Discovering the Future* (St. Paul, MN: ILI Press, 1989), 42.

7. Aubrey Malphurs, *Doing Church* (Grand Rapids: Kregel, 1999).

8. Collins and Lazier, *Beyond Entrepreneurship*, 199.

9. Ibid., 200–202.

10. Ibid., 203.

11. Kouzes and Posner, *The Leadership Challenge*, 44.

12. Ken Blanchard, "Personal Excellence in the 21st Century," *Forum Files* 4, no. 3 (August 1994).

13. Ken Blanchard and Michael O'Connor, *Managing by Values* (San Francisco: Berrett-Koehler, 1997), 31, 45, 108, 121.

14. Eliza G. Collins, *Executive Success: Making It in Management* (New York: John Wiley and Sons, 1985), 210.

Chapter 7 How Not to Drop the Ball

1. Jim Collins, "Aligning Action and Values," *Leader to Leader* 1 (summer 1996), 4.

2. Thomas R. Horton, *What Works for Me* (New York: Random House, 1986), 28–29.

3. Jim Collins addresses this in more detail in his article "Aligning Actions and Values."

INDEX

Megliano, Bruce, 41
Merck and Company, 161, 163
ministry
    chaos in, 52–53
    character of, 23–25
    creativity in, 21
    distinctives of, 14–15
    expense of, 25–26
    involvement in, 16
    motivation in, 21–22
    new, 119
    participation, 21
    performance, 25–26
    personal, 26
    success in, 25–26
    values and, 10, 23–26, 30, 37–53,
        57–58, 119–27
    vision in, 9–10, 27
ministry awareness, 170
morale, 172
Morris, Linus, 137
motivation, 170

Northwood Community Church (Dallas),
    145, 151–52

O'Connor, Michael, 126
O'Reilly, Charles, 38
organizational context, 170
organizational hierarchy, 171
organizational structure, 171
organizational values, 9–10, 18–19, 44,
    134

paradigm effect, 121
Parkview Evangelical Free Church (Iowa
    City, IA), 86, 145, 153
pastor. See also leadership
    appointing of, 63–64
    candidating of, 16, 64
    leadership stages and, 116–17
    values casting by, 136–37, 143
personal values, 49, 50, 57, 60–62, 75
personnel management, 18–19
Peters, Tom, 9, 47, 108
Porras, Jerry, 82
Posner, Barry Z., 22, 47, 107, 109
prayer, 42–43, 70, 71
prior change, 171–72
priorities
    core values and, 17–18, 40, 61, 83

determination of, 43
single value and, 51
problem solving, 42–43
processes/functions, 170
programming, 105
psychographics, 117

reality, 32
recruiting, 137–38
rewards, 171
risk taking, 43–44
Rokeach, Milton, 31
RTS Bulletin (Reformed Theological Sem-
    inary), 104
rural areas, 117–18

Saddleback Valley Community Church
    (Mission Viejo, CA), 82, 83, 84, 86,
    145, 153
Schaller, Lyle, 13, 14, 20, 40
Schooler, C., 68
secularism, 36
self-evaluation, 61–62
Sonlife Ministries (Wheaton, IL), 157
staff relations, 17
strategies, 31
success, 25–26
Swindoll, Charles, 22, 97

theology of excellence, 24–25
Tillapaugh, Frank, 118
traditions, 120–21
truth, 36

Unleashing the Church (Tillapaugh), 118
urban areas, 117–18

values. See also core values
    actual, 50–51
    aspirational, 50–51
    clear, 88
    conflicting, 52–53
    congruent, 25, 52–53
    conscious, 46–47
    correction of, 139–42
    defending, 141–42
    development of, 75–89
    enforcing of, 140–41
    incongruent, 52–53
    maintenance of, 120–21
    modeling of, 122–23, 135–36

Aubrey Malphurs is a professor of pastoral ministries at Dallas Seminary and the president of The Malphurs Group. He is available for consultation on various topics related to leadership, vision, church planting, and church renewal. Those wishing to contact him for consulting or speaking engagements may do so through The Malphurs Group, 7916 Briar Brook Court, Dallas, TX 75218; 214-841-3777; aubrey@malphursgroup.com; www.malphursgroup.com.